Moving in Faith, Taking Off the Robes

(Women's Bible Study)

by
Jennifer Kostyal

Names of perpetrators have been changed in incidents that are shared.

Moving in Faith, Taking Off the Robes
(Women's Bible Study)
Copyright © 2005
ISBN 0-88144-226-7
Jennifer Kostyal
Transformed By the Word Ministries
P. O. Box 10141
Wilmington, NC 28404
910/686-7265
transformedbytheword.org

Published by
Rutherford Resources LLC
55550 E. 265 Rd
Afton, OK 74331

rutherfordresources@wavelinx.net
www.rutherfordresources.com

Cover and Text Design: Bobby and Lisa Simpson
www.SimpsonProductions.net

Dedication

I dedicate this work to all the women who are going to receive freedom by completing this Bible study. Through the blood of Jesus, you will be released from the damage the enemy has done in your life. I love you and I cannot wait to see you walk into your new life with your beautiful "robe of righteousness."

Contents

Required Bibles to Do the Study:
    New King James Version
    Amplified Bible

Acknowledgments

To my wonderful husband, Dave, you are so amazing and I love you dearly. You have been my "knight in shining armor" from Jesus! Thanks for all the "pep talks" to never give up. David II and Rebekah, you are such beautiful gifts from Jesus. Mommy thanks you for sharing me with those who are hurting and need Jesus. I praise Jesus for giving me the family I always dreamed of having. Dave, David, and Rebekah, you really do make me smile! I am such a blessed woman to have you to spend my life with as we walk in our destinies with Jesus.

To Rev. and Mrs. Roy Belon, I love you and I thank you for being the best Mom and Dad I could ever have! To God be the glory for your compassion to a broken college student at UNC that you adopted and believed could be healed.

To my Pastors, John and Brenda McEntee, you are truly the best pastors anyone could have to learn about faith. Thank you for your support and prayers. I love you both deeply.

To Trianna Kirkland, you are my big sister. Thanks for all of your love and advice. "Tri," you helped me keep going and always believed in the dream. I love you dearly.

To my incredible staff, I love you and appreciate all of you listening and praying for me. To Lori Capace, you are a blessing from heaven. Thank you for keeping me organized. To Donna Vaughan, your love for Jesus is a joy. To Katie Furr, you are such an anointed singer and I love your energy for Jesus.

Prayer for a Personal Relationship with the Lord

God wants you to receive His free gift of salvation. Jesus wants to save you and fill you with the Holy Spirit more than anything. If you have never invited Jesus, the Prince of Peace, to be your Lord and Savior, I invite you to do so now. Pray the following prayer, and if you are really sincere about it, you will experience a new life in Christ.

Father, You loved the world so much, You gave Your only begotten Son to die for our sins so whoever believes in Him will not perish but have eternal life.

Your Word says we are saved by grace through faith as a gift from You. There is nothing we can do to earn salvation.

I believe and confess with my mouth that Jesus Christ is Your Son, the Savior of the world. I believe He died on the cross for me and bore all of my sins, paying the price for them. I believe in my heart that You raised Jesus from the dead.

I ask You to forgive my sins. I confess Jesus as my Lord. According to Your Word, I am saved and will spend eternity with You! Thank You, Father. I am so grateful! In Jesus' name. Amen.

(See John 3:16; Ephesians 2:8-9; Romans 10:9-10; 1 Corinthians 15:3-4; 1 John 1:9, 4:14-16, 5:1,12-13.)

Foreword

It is not by coincidence that you have chosen to participate in this life transforming Bible Study, ***Moving in Faith, Taking off the Robes.*** In fact, God has chosen YOU to journey alongside thousands of women who share in brokenness and are in need of healing and becoming all that God desires you to be.

This Bible study is part of Jennifer Kostyal's compelling and miraculous testimony of God's transforming power in her life. Jennifer unselfishly shares her childhood pain, trauma, and suffering and emerged as a gifted writer and evangelist who invites thousands to hope that Christ alone provides. Jennifer is a living witness who is clothed with the full armor of God, whose joy and deep love for her Savior is overflowing to all who are blessed to know her. Her deepest desire and God's will for you is to be freed from emotional pain, bondage, strongholds, low self-esteem, and to ultimately be transformed by the grace of God.

Jennifer so beautifully uses the analogy and illustration of "taking off the robes" of fear, unforgiveness, religion and tradition, negative words and complaining, judgment and criticism, and rejection and leads you to accept the robe of righteousness. Through the daily assignments, scripture verses and Biblical truths, you will have the opportunity to face your deepest fears and irrational beliefs that Satan would have you believe. Next, she has you acknowledge what hinders you from becoming the Godly woman that God so desires for you, and replace them with God's truths. As you exchange the robes, you will become transformed to a new life in Christ in right standing with God. ***Moving in Faith, Taking off the Robes*** is truly life changing!

As a Christ-centered licensed professional counselor, I am dedicated to serving others in Godly ways, integrating Biblical truths with the well proven mental health practices. Day in and day out in my practice, I hear and see brokenness that only God can heal. As clients reveal their pain, fears, sins, and hopelessness, I share in Jennifer's love and compassion for those who are in need of hope and healing. This Bible study leads others towards Christ for forgiveness, healing and ultimately restoration. I am blessed to be able to use this Bible study as a resource in my counseling practice.

It is a true blessing to know Jennifer Kostyal and to have benefited personally from her Bible study and to be able to share ***Moving in Faith, Taking off the Robes*** with others. I highly recommend it without reservation. Enjoy your journey to wholeness and may God bless you as you are transformed by the Word!

Joanne G. Davenport, MA, CAS, NCC, LPC
Licensed Professional Counselor
Wilmington, NC

Preface

Evangelist Jennifer Kostyal is a modern-day Moses, Paul, and Esther. She is the total embodiment of the faith and witness of these three great biblical influences.

Moses (or more appropriately, Mosetta) best describes this female Emancipator. Like Moses, she has led and pioneered her people to freedom or to the promised land. Her people are all people: males, females, poor, rich, learned, unlearned, all races, all religions, and all ages. Her mission is not discriminating, thus it is welcomed by all. To know this anointed woman of God is to have a foretaste of glory divine. She is a modern lawgiver, like Moses, who not only knows the Scriptures and can teach them, but she practices what she teaches and preaches.

Her Damascus road experience was similar to Paul's. God reached down and anointed her for His service, just as He did Paul. A past of dejection, alienation from God, incest and sexual abuse, rejection by family, depression, low self-esteem, feelings of inferiority, dreadful nightmares, insecurities, and delusions all plagued this vessel who was to be used by God.

After the scales fell from her eyes, like Paul, she has gone about her Father's business. As Paul was a prolific writer of the New Testament, so Jennifer has launched her career as a modern-day scribe. This initial work is only the tip of the iceberg that represents what God has to say to the world through her.

Lastly, my friend Jennifer "has come to the whole world for such a time as this." Like Esther, Jennifer is a leader and a revolutionist. Like Esther, her physical beauty radiates an inner beauty that is phenomenal. As Esther won the heart of the king, Jennifer has landed a husband, David, who is her greatest supporter and advisor. He is her lifelong soul mate and encourager.

In a world torn by such chaos as war, drugs, terrorism, unrest, deceit, infidelity, divorce, child abuse, incest, pornography, atheism, dysfunctional families, and treachery, Jennifer in this book offers hope, peace, contentment, and unconditional love as she leads the way to a Savior of whom it is said in Hebrews 4:15, "[He] was in all points tempted as we are, yet without sin." Christ knows all about our temptations and struggles.

In this book, Jennifer disrobes us of our hang-ups and at the conclusion of this masterful work, when we view ourselves in the mirror, we see a finished product of what happens when we have been with Jesus. (Acts 4:13.)

To edit this inspiring book has been a privilege and a pleasure. I have been impacted by the awesome experience that the reading of this great book has proved to be, and I trust Jennifer will give me many opportunities again to "sit at her feet" as I testify and witness to the wisdom of a great, yet humble, woman of God.

Your fellow believer, sister, and friend,

Rev. Dr. Lydia Aiken Wilson

Introduction

When the Lord spoke to me many months ago and told me to write a Bible study, I waited to hear from Him as to what to write about. I would not venture to do this without the Holy Spirit guiding me, because I know that by myself this venture would fail. I have never seen myself as a writer, but the Holy Spirit spoke to me and told me He would help me.

I will never forget the day I called Dr. Lydia Wilson, one of my college professors, and asked her if she would edit my work on a Bible study that the Holy Spirit had prompted me to write. She embraced me and said, "Whatever you need me to do I will do it, because Jennifer, you can do this."

These words were music to my ears and I cried to think someone I respected as I did Dr. Wilson would help me. I am so amazed at how God can take a little broken girl from Bolivia, North Carolina, who was raised down a road called "Mud" and use her.

During my life I have worn many robes of many kinds. Even as a child, I just took any old robe and wore it, pretending it was the princess robe I had been dreaming of wearing. Throughout the past ten years of my life, the Holy Spirit has been stripping me of all of the robes which man had placed upon me. This process has been very painful at times. It was consoling to read recently in Psalms that my Father in heaven places all of my tears in His bottle: **"You number and record my wanderings; put my tears into Your bottle – are they not in Your book?"** (Psalm 56:8 AMP). Isn't it amazing to realize that God knows all of the tears you have ever shed? You have never been alone and never will be with Jesus Christ by your side.

My dear sisters in Christ, we all wear robes that we have grown so accustomed to that we do not realize they have been placed upon our very beings. At the age of four, I found out what wearing the robe of perversion was when a member of my extended family started to sexually molest me for a period of over ten years. The enemy then came in to place upon me many robes I thought were part of who I was.

Often, I heard what my biological parents said over me as a little child — that I was always so nervous and they thought it was simply how I was. No, being nervous was not my personality. I lived in constant anxiety due to my life of sexual abuse that was a secret between me and another member of my family.

Today, when I look at my beautiful daughter Rebekah, I smile deeply as I see her in princess dress-up clothes feeling so beautiful and adored by my husband Dave and me.

As a child I always felt ugly and rejected. I remember standing in the bathroom on my honeymoon night in a beautiful white gown knowing I did not deserve to wear it because my innocence had been removed at a very young age. Dave always tried to make me feel beautiful, but there were so many secrets he did not know about. However, I played the games of marriage and motherhood as best I could and tried to forget all of the ugly memories that were so deep inside of me.

At the age of thirty, after the birth of my daughter Rebekah, I became so depressed that life did not seem worth living as I was forced to look at some ugly robes I thought I had covered with a few of life's accomplishments. I sincerely praise Jesus for His grace and love to help me get out of clothes that I was never supposed to wear.

Come on this journey with me for the next seven weeks and let's depend upon the Word, the Holy Spirit, and God the Father to take off our robes so we can walk hand in hand on this journey called life.

Through the power of God's Word, I can now look into the mirror and not see the sad little girl that no one noticed was crying out for help, but a woman who realizes she has a Daddy in heaven who loves her and is smiling.

You will shed tears as you embrace this Bible study, but remember, your Daddy in heaven will be gathering them in His bottle to give them back as sweet perfume when He converts your tears into joy!

SUGGESTED GUIDELINES FOR BIBLE STUDY LEADERS

Introductory Session

GOALS AS LEADERS

- ❑ Welcome and hug each member. Remember, we all need to be loved.

- ❑ Register each member.

- ❑ Get phone numbers and addresses of each member.

- ❑ Pass out books and get payment. Allow them to pay the following week if necessary.

- ❑ Explain the Bible study and how you were prompted to start this study.

- ❑ Explain to your members that next week you will be discussing Week One of the study so they need to do the five devotionals for Week One to be prepared. However, tell them not to miss the Bible study group simply because they have not done the work. Impress upon them that they will enjoy the fellowship and they can always catch up on the work.

Suggested Outline for Your Weekly Meetings

I recommend small groups with up to twelve women. If you have a few more or less, that is fine. However, if you have chosen this study for your church, I recommend small groups of twelve women and a group leader for each one. Within a church setting you may choose one woman to head up the Bible study and meet together as a large group for a twenty-five- to thirty-minute large group introduction and then assign small group leaders as recommended.

The church can have a sign-up for the Bible study and have your women's leader organize the study. Every week have the women meet together as a large group for a synopsis of the study, then dismiss into small groups of twelve or less women as assigned by the leader.

Suggested Itinerary for Introduction of Small Groups

1. Open with prayer and prayer requests.

2. During first week, have women in their small groups introduce themselves. Please make them feel comfortable by first introducing yourself.

3. Explain how the enemy does not want them to finish this study and that you will be praying for them. Tell them that the time needed to do the study will be worth it and that you will be praying for them daily.

4. Explain that you will be choosing some of the questions from each day's devotional of the week they are studying and that you will be discussing them as part of a small group. Explain that they will never have to answer personal questions if they do not feel comfortable and that all discussion is voluntary.

5. Emphasize the need to be present at the weekly meeting for fellowship and prayer time.

6. Have all the ladies in your small group give you their address and phone numbers.

Proposed Order of Weekly Meetings

1. Women's leader of church gives a one twenty-five- to thirty-minute synopsis of the week's lesson, prays with the women, then dismisses them into small groups. Also, you may want some praise and worship before your women's leader addresses the large group.

2. Small groups:

   * Welcome your sisters in Christ (3-5 minutes).

   * Prayer requests (write down the requests) and have prayer time with group. The leader should lead the prayer (10 minutes).

   * Discuss the week's lesson by choosing at least two questions for your group from each day's lesson. Let the Holy Spirit lead you. Keep women focused on the Bible study and questions asked within the study (30 minutes).

   * End with prayer for your group's week and each woman's time with the Lord within the study (5 minutes).

   * Speak with your women individually and send them on their way with a hug and words of encouragement (5 minutes).

PROPOSED THINGS THE LEADER SHOULD DO
FOR MEMBERS OF SMALL GROUP

1. Call the members of your small group and check on their weekly progress.

2. Send the women of your group cards of encouragement once or twice during the seven weeks of the study.

3. If any women in your group miss a week, call them and let them know they were missed. See if you can do anything to get them back for the next week's session.

4. Encourage your group members to pray for each other every day during these seven weeks.

NOTE TO BIBLE STUDY LEADERS

Leading a women's Bible study will be one of the most rewarding things you will ever do in the Kingdom of God. I am so proud of you for moving in faith and allowing the Lord to use you to help His daughters.

The enemy will try to attack you during this Bible study, and I want to remind you to plead the blood of Jesus daily over you and your family and remember that the devil is under your feet. (Colossians 2:15.)

You will be rewarded as you help women learn more about the Word of God. Women love to come to Bible studies, and they will appreciate you doing the same order of things weekly so they can discuss their answers.

However, always be sensitive to the Holy Spirit. There may be weeks when the time for prayer requests will be longer. Always discuss the week's lesson and cover questions, enabling the women to learn from each other. It is helpful for women to know they are not alone in dealing with the issues of their lives.

I love you and know you will love leading your sisters in Christ as they begin moving in faith and taking off the robes.

Your sister in Christ,

Jennifer

Suggested Guidelines for Independent Study

You will benefit from this study, even if you do not have a women's group to be a part of, and you work it independently.

Allow the same length of time to complete the study — seven weeks — so you have time to meditate upon the Word and the principles presented in each lesson. Yield yourself totally to the work of the Holy Spirit. Let Him reveal issues to you that need to be dealt with, and let Him become your **"Comforter (Counselor, Helper, Intercessor, Advocate, Strengthener, and Standby)"** as John 14:16 AMP states. He is also your **"Spirit of Truth"** (v. 17).

As you are diligent to complete this study, you will never be the same. You will be further transformed into the image and likeness of Jesus Christ!

Your sister in Christ,

Jennifer

Week 1

"Help, I'm scared!"

I sought (inquired of) the Lord and required of Him
[of necessity and on the authority of His Word], and He heard me,
and delivered me from all my fears.
Psalm 34:4 AMP

The holidays were in full swing and life was good. How blessed my life had been since I became a Christian. My heart was at peace as I sat next to my husband, Dave, and glanced across the aisle at our two beautiful children, David and Rebekah. Although Dave knew that I didn't care for flying, he had reasoned that the twelve-hour drive to see his parents in Pennsylvania would be hard on our young children. Put that way, it only made sense to fly and I agreed.

So far, so good, I thought as the final passengers boarded. Then … I heard the door to the aircraft shut. Suddenly my peace shattered. My heart began to race and I became terrified that I was being shut in and could not get out! Intending to reach for the Bible in my lap, I gripped Dave's arm. My eyes filled with tears as I quietly pleaded, "Dave I *have* to get off this plane. Please get me out."

For years I had simply avoided flying. In the few instances when it became necessary, I made sure that I had enough alcohol in my system to deaden the panicky feeling of being shut in. Little did I realize, I was actually shutting down my emotions by this abuse of alcohol. I know now that drinking is never the answer. The relief it brings is only temporary, and it can take the abuser down a very slippery slope of destruction.

This day on the plane, however, caught me off guard. The fact that I had been a Christian for many years and was even a minister of the Gospel had led me to believe that the panic attacks were a thing of the past. Was I ever wrong! Once again that old enemy held me captive in his terrifying grip. My mind raced back to my honeymoon trip with Dave. Back then, not wanting him to find out that I had to have a drink in order to board a plane, I pretended to be concerned about the high cost of airfare. It was a very poor argument since he was quite well off financially; nevertheless, I persuaded him to drive us to Charleston. Through manipulation I was able to avoid the problem.

This time, however, there was no avoiding it. I was thrown into an emotional tailspin and couldn't conceal it from Dave. Wisely, instead of taking me off the plane, he firmly but lovingly encouraged me to do what he had seen me do for years to combat the devil's attacks. He was referring to how I had learned to overcome the demonic lies that had been sown in my life through years of abuse during my childhood. Pointing to the Bible on my lap, he simply said, "Jennifer, you know what to do."

I knew he was right. Although the fear was suffocating, his words sparked a bit of courage in me. With the help of the Holy Spirit, the Word of God, and Jesus, I knew I could overcome. I opened my Bible to 2 Timothy 1:7 and began reading the words that had become so familiar to me: "For God has not given us a spirit of fear, but of power and of love and of a sound mind."

As I turned my focus to Jesus and allowed the words of this scripture to penetrate my heart, the calm that I had become accustomed to once again enveloped me. Then, as the jet started down the runway, I kissed my Bible and laid my head on Dave's shoulder. Although I cannot say that I enjoyed that flight or the return trip, it was a turning point for me. For the first time, I was able to experience some measure of victory over that paralyzing fear.

Obviously, Dave played a significant role in my victory that day, and I am forever grateful to the Lord for this godly man. Two of the things I appreciate the most about him are that he loves Jesus with his whole heart and he constantly points me to the Word of God, reminding me to take every problem to the Lord Jesus. By doing this, Dave is following the example set by the apostle Paul when he told the church at Ephesus to "take the helmet of salvation, and the sword of the Spirit, which is the word of God" (Eph. 6:17). The truth is, you and I can destroy every demonic, oppressive spirit of fear by using the Word of God and by "praying always with all prayer and supplication in the Spirit, being watchful" (Eph. 6:18).

That day on the plane was victory for me, but even more importantly, I knew the time had come for me to face head-on whatever had been giving that spirit of fear access to my life. Jesus said, "The thief does not come except to steal, and to kill, and to destroy. I have come that they may have life, and that they may have it more abundantly" (John 10:10). That spirit of fear had been putting a damper on the abundant life Jesus purchased for me every time I entered an elevator, an airplane, a closet, or any other space that made me feel closed in. Psychologists call it *claustrophobia,* but I knew from reading the Bible that I did not have to accept it because Jesus paid the price for my freedom. He said, "And you shall know the truth, and the truth shall make you free" (John 8:32). I was tired of watching other people—even unbelievers—do the things I wanted to do but wouldn't even attempt because fear held me back. I was determined to overcome this fear once and for all.

THE ROOT REVEALED

As I sought the Lord in earnest about the paralyzing claustrophobia, the Holy Spirit began to reveal when the spirit of fear had entered my life. He reminded me of the many times a family member, Scott, had locked me inside a large silo used to store corn on our family farm. These traumatic "shut in" moments began when I was about five years old. Because both of my parents worked, they left me alone with Scott for many hours at a time during the summer. When he would practice his cruelty, I would beg him to let me out, but he always refused. The sound of his laughter was haunting, the pitch-black dark terrifying. I will never forget the sound of the metal door being closed and the long metal rod sliding into place to keep the door firmly locked. What had been meant to secure the corn in a dry environment was used to hold me prisoner. No wonder the sound of the jet door being closed had affected me in such a powerful way.

To further increase my terror, Scott would then run around the huge metal structure, beating it with a tobacco stick and screaming that there were snakes inside ready to bite me. I learned over time that my only ticket to freedom was to quit screaming and begging, regardless of how terrified I was. Only then would my captor open the huge metal door so I could escape. Then I would run with all my might to the house and shut myself up in my bedroom to calm down. Often I would break out in hives due to an allergic reaction to the corn dust and had to take a bath and change clothes. The whole ordeal would leave me feeling exhausted and hopeless.

You might ask, "Why didn't you just tell your parents?" Actually, I did, but they insisted that I was lying. The reason was that Scott was held in very high esteem by my parents—and our community. Marked for leadership in the religious group we belonged to, he could do no wrong in their eyes. When I finally realized that it was useless to cry out for help, I simply shut down and carried my pain in silence—alone.

THE TRUTH SET ME FREE

Now that the Lord had revealed how the spirit of fear had come into my life, I knew that only the Word of God and prayer could defeat and eradicate it. One weekend when Dave happened to be out of town on a business trip, I felt strongly that I was to invite a dear friend and several prayer warriors to my house to help me walk my road to freedom. Although Dave was not able to be with us in person, he prayed with me over the telephone before and after the prayer session. Another friend agreed to keep my children so that my prayer partners and I could have the house to ourselves.

Although I could have done this alone, I knew there was power in the prayer of agreement and that Jesus had sent out His disciples in pairs to minister. (See Matt. 18:19; Mark 6:7.) In my case, the devil had tried to convince me that if I ever revisited those memories of the silo I would lose my mind. Having the support of committed prayer warriors helped to put those fears to rest. I know now that Satan threatened my sanity so that I would not defeat him at his ugly game.

As these dear prayer partners and I began to pray, peace filled the room and the Holy Spirit accompanied me back to that pitch-black corn silo. There, in my heart, I saw Jesus Himself holding me and comforting me. It was then that He had enabled me to quiet my screams, so my tormentor would let me go. Much to the devil's chagrin, I did not lose my mind, but I finally saw the situation for what it was. That fear of being locked up was turned into a tremendous revelation of knowing that no matter how bad a situation is, Jesus is always there and He can make it right.

Once the light of Truth was shined on those times of darkness, I could see how the devil had used circumstances in my adult life to trigger those same horrifying feelings over and over to torment me. But that day it ended. Sure, thoughts of fear still try to attack me from time to time, but they no longer have power over me. Now I know the truth, and it has set me free, just as Jesus promised.

EACH HEALING JOURNEY IS UNIQUE

It is not always necessary to revisit traumatic events or bring blocked memories back to life, but that is how the Lord has chosen to bring about my healing. However He does it, it is important to note that He will only begin when the timing is right. He will never force you to look at a situation before you are ready. It is also crucial that you be built up spiritually. Fasting and spending much time in the Word of God and prayer are ways to prepare your heart for the healing process. It is then that you can most effectively be led by the Spirit on the healing journey that He has custom designed for you. In my case, the flight on the airplane signaled to me that it was time to receive healing for that area of my life. I was desperate, and I knew I was ready.

Wherever your path to freedom takes you, it is important to understand that healing doesn't usually take place all at once. Most often it is a process of growing from glory to glory. It is also needful to remember that the devil is persistent. He will try to attack you again, but as you continue to stand on the Word of God, you will have the power to resist those spirits and they will flee from you. (See James 4:7.)

As I have shared, God brought some wonderful prayer partners into my life to help me wage war on the spirit of fear. Although you can certainly receive healing alone with the Father, the prayer support of fellow believers is one of the functions of the Body of Christ. There is simply added power when we link arms together in prayer. Deuteronomy 32:30 says, "How could one chase a thousand, and two put ten thousand to flight, unless their Rock had sold them, and the LORD had surrendered them?"

If you do not feel that there is anyone in your life at present to pray the prayer of agreement with you, ask the Lord to meet this legitimate need. Amos 3:3 says, "Can two walk together, unless they are agreed?" God wants you to have people in your life who are of like precious faith. As you join together, the mountains that have stood in the way of your freedom will have to begin to move.

BE ENCOURAGED

My sweet sister in Christ, let me tell you the truth about the situations in your life that have clothed you in fear and have caused you such distress. Jesus was there standing for you in ways you cannot imagine. In fact, I believe He is saying to you the same thing that he said to His disciple, Simon Peter: "Indeed, Satan has asked for you, that he may sift you as wheat. But I have prayed for you, that your faith should not fail" (Luke 22:31–32). The fact that you are reading this now is proof that the Father has answered Jesus' prayer for you. I encourage you to thank Him right now for keeping you and for bringing you this far. But this is only the beginning. Know assuredly that Jesus will deliver you of *all* your fears so that you can stand before Him totally free.

Jeremiah 17:14 has been a great encouragement to me, and I believe it will fill you with hope as well. It says, "Heal me, O LORD, and I shall be healed; save me, and I shall be saved, for You are my praise." The Lord heard this cry of my heart and I know He hears yours too. Together we can spend eternity thanking Him for releasing you from the prison of fear!

No matter how impossible it seems to you, know assuredly that you are already on the road to freedom. Horrifying memories will become a thing of the past through the power of the Word of God and the blood of Jesus. The Holy Spirit revealed to me during my healing process that He is intimately acquainted with every detail of our lives. Where our soul realm (our mind, will, and emotions) have been damaged, He pours in the healing "balm of Gilead" (Jeremiah 8:22). Life becomes peaceful as He ministers to us, which in turn enables us to view the circumstances of our past differently. Suddenly the pain that once kept us from visiting the abuses and wrongs of the past is gone, anesthetized by the power of the Holy Spirit. We can still remember the events but no longer feel any pain!

Whether it has been in person or via the many forms of media available today, the Lord has graciously given me the opportunity to share my healing from rape, molestation, and religious abuse with people all over the world. I no longer sob uncontrollably when I tell my story, as I did before receiving my healing, because the Holy Spirit has given me the power to share it without feeling the immense pain. I liken it to looking at the scar below my left knee, which came from a surgery I had while in the eighth grade. The scar is still visible, but I no longer feel the pain that I did for two weeks after the operation. In the same way, the emotional scars of my life have been removed by the blood of Jesus. Now, even though I can remember the abusive situations, the pain is gone. Praise the Lord!

Dear sister, your time of deliverance is here! Know that as you seek your Heavenly Father for help, He will in no way deny you or your request. Let Jesus be the answer you have cried out for. He has never refused even one of His girls, and He is waiting with open arms to receive you now. One of the reasons He died upon the cross was so that you could live a peaceful life, free from the robe of fear that has been placed upon you through the afflictions of this life. And remember, He triumphed over the author of fear—Satan—so you can be completely delivered. You have His Word on it.

Join me now for this week's Bible study. Day by day, we will walk through practical steps so that you can remove the paralyzing robe of fear once and for all. As you begin, be encouraged by the words of Jesus: "Do not fear, little flock, for it is your Father's good pleasure to give you the kingdom" (Luke 12:32).

Week 1

Take Off the Robe of Fear

Week 1, Day 1 — You Are Accepted in the Beloved

My dear sisters in Christ, welcome to a deep and exciting study of the Word of God. I have found in my own personal life that when God causes me to study His Word, I am being transformed into the image of His Son, Jesus Christ.

You will find yourself facing much needed truths as we venture into the undressing room of the Most High God. As one who has already been stripped of ugly robes, do not run away when you feel as though things are getting tough. When you are finished with this study, you will be amazed at how beautiful you look as you walk down the aisle with your gorgeous robe of righteousness to truly see Jesus in a new light.

Stay with me as we travel on a journey that will transform you into the Bride of Christ you have always dreamed of becoming. I cannot help but think of one of my favorite Bible verses that served to change my life: **"But seek first the kingdom of God and His righteousness, and all these things shall be added to you"** (Matthew 6:33).

What is your definition of "fear"?

_____

_____

What do you fear the most? (You may have more than one fear.) This is a robe that you need to face and remove.

_____

_____

_____

_____

Holman's Bible Dictionary defines "fear" as follows:

A broad range of emotions that embrace both the secular and the religious worlds. Secular fear is the natural feeling of alarm caused by the expectation of imminent danger, pain, or disaster. Religious fear appears as the result of awe and reverence toward a supreme power.[1]

Something happened recently as I was leaving my son David's ball game that literally made me run to the computer the next morning to ask the Holy Spirit to anoint me as I continued to write this study.

---

[1]*Holman's Bible Dictionary* (Nashville, TN: Holman Bible Publishers, 1991), 480.

My husband Dave, my daughter Rebekah, David, and I were leaving David's minor league ball game. As we walked to the parking lot, a woman of about thirty-five years of age approached Dave and me and asked Dave for a tissue. Dave looked at me so she turned and asked me the same question. When I looked into her eyes, I saw sorrow and pain. I walked up very close to her and said, "Are you all right?"

This woman started pouring out how her mom had died and her brother, who had been diagnosed with Down's syndrome at a young age, was now in a nursing home. I noticed immediately the smell of alcohol on her breath, but I did not blink or back off. You see, I used to hide my pains in a bottle of beer, and I'm sure many people smelled my breath as I did this woman's.

I hugged her close and told her I loved her and so did Jesus. She apologized for the smell of alcohol and I told her that I used to wear that same robe to hide my pain. She cried and we said a prayer right in the middle of that parking lot, surrounded by smiling people leaving the game with their children in tow.

This woman's last comment to me made me shudder. She asked me not to tell anyone about the alcohol because of her husband's business associations in the neighboring town. Her robe was becoming more noticeable, and I believe I gave it a tug with a simple prayer and a hug.

Many times we look at women and think they have everything under control when they are actually barely making it underneath their robes of country club membership, church membership, academic success, addictions, fake smiles, overprotective mothering, gossip, beautiful clothing and accessories, and many more.

Let's turn to the book of Exodus and examine the life of an Old Testament woman whom we do not hear much about. However, we see entire books of the Bible that her son wrote. The woman is Jochebed.

Read Exodus 1:8-2:9.

What strikes you about how the midwives reacted to Pharaoh's command? Use Exodus 1:21 to help you answer.

_____

_____

_____

_____

Whom, other than God, do you fear at home, at work, in your friendships? (Note: Your "fear of God" is a reverential fear.)

_____

_____

Are you being submissive to God's Word or to man's?

_____

_____

_____

What do you think the Scriptures mean in Exodus 2:2 where it was said that Moses was *beautiful?*

_____

_____

_____

End today's lesson by reading Malachi 3:16. You will experience this message when you meet in your small groups. God Almighty is listening to you discuss His power and love toward you. Be real in these small groups and let your sisters help you remove your robes.

The fear of God is a beautiful feeling of security and love. Many of us do not have those fond childhood memories of a daddy loving and accepting us. You do not have to fear, because you are accepted by your Daddy in heaven.

Take a moment and thank God for loving you no matter what you have done wrong. His love will not change. He will not leave you or forsake you. (Deuteronomy 31:6.) Rest in His arms and weep as you face the truth: You have fear and you want it taken off during the next four days of this Bible study.

Hang in there with me and you will make it to the end and get your bottle of perfume.

Meditate on this verse the rest of the day:

"Be strong and of good courage, do not fear nor be afraid of them; for the Lord your God, He is the One who goes with you. He will not leave you nor forsake you" (Deuteronomy 31:6).

Week 1, Day 2 — Visit the Nile

Yesterday we discussed and realized that we all have fears. Whenever we look at this woman named Jochebed, we can imagine that, as a slave and mother, she had many fears.

Can you imagine Jochebed pregnant with her baby and then at birth realizing she had a beautiful baby boy? Moses was her dream child and she refused to be scared of Pharaoh or his command to throw all the baby boys in Egypt into the Nile.

During Old Testament times, the Pharaohs were the most powerful people in the world. They were looked upon as gods. Jochebed knew that her God, Yahweh, was stronger than Pharaoh and figured out a way to hide her precious baby boy. According to the Scripture, she built an ark and placed him in it.

What is in your life that you cannot hide any longer? God is asking you to step out in faith and believe His Word over your fears.

_____

_____

_____

_____

What are you building to place your children, marriage, or dreams in when the fear of the enemy comes upon you?

_____

_____

_____

_____

If you are using anything other than the Word of God to be your ark, you are destined for a fall. You may look like you are being successful; however, things will eventually get too tough. When we are in love with Jesus, we are in love with the Word of God. You may ask how am I able to make such a statement. I base this statement on John 1:14: **"And the Word became flesh and dwelt among us, and we beheld His glory, the glory as of the only begotten of the Father, full of grace and truth."**

Write out 1 John 5:7:

_____

_____

As American women, it is hard for us to imagine the fear brought upon a mother faced with having to place her baby in the Nile. The Nile River had the dreaded Nile crocodile, and for Jochebed to place her son in the very place that Pharaoh was commanding his soldiers to throw all the boy babies required amazing faith. This act placed her among the "Heroes of Faith" noted by the Apostle Paul.

Jochebed was a woman of fearless confidence and courage in God's ability to save her offspring. I love the way her lineage is noted when she is mentioned in Exodus 2:1. Jochebed was of the tribe of Levi. She understood the Abrahamic covenant under which her children were covered.

Read Genesis 22:18, Deuteronomy 28:1-14, Psalm 112:2, and Galatians 3:29. What promise do you have to claim over your children or your life as you walk with God?

_____

_____

_____

_____

Jesus often taught the people that they had to believe in order to receive the promises of God. My dear sisters, so do you. You have to know it is the will of God to bless you and your household. If Jochebed had not known she was under the covenant of God, she would have moved in fear and would never have hidden Moses for three months.

When Moses became too loud, she did not fret; she placed her baby in an ark. Jochebed could have become very fearful when she could not keep her baby quiet. However, instead, she started building an ark. This woman had a promise and she acted in faith, not fear.

Read Hebrews 11:23. How did the parents of Moses "move" to decide to come against Pharaoh's command?

_____

_____

Give your definition of "faith":

_____

_____

Write out Hebrews 11:1 AMP:

_____

_____

_____

_____

My sisters, fear is the exact opposite of faith. Whenever we are moving in fear or dealing with fear, we have left God out of the equation. Remember, faith is the substance of things hoped for, the evidence of things we can't see. Get rid of your reasoning and move in faith. Fear is a spirit of the enemy and it stops so many of us in our tracks.

Write out 2 Timothy 1:7:

_____

_____

God sent His Son, Jesus, to die on the cross so we do not have to be afraid. This is a new life for me, and it is truly an abundant life. Let me explain by sharing my personal example of how the spirit of fear was closing in on me at every angle. I am sure that many of you have not experienced such dreaded fear; however, I am going to share "my story" with you as the Holy Spirit has directed me to do.

When my life fell apart at age thirty, I started having anxiety attacks off and on during the night as well as during the day. Because of the anxiety attacks, I started envisioning awful things happening to my baby and toddler. Eventually, it became a struggle to even go outside with them to play. My whole life was shutting down, and I did not know I could turn to the Word of God and be saved from this awful spirit of fear.

God sent many people into my life who told me about Jesus and about standing on the promises of the Word of God. Little by little, I was delivered from awful fears too gruesome to even relate. For many hours, I would walk the floor and hold the Bible and say the Bible verses out loud that dealt with fear. I am not exaggerating, my sisters. Fear began to leave and the world started to look different.

Whatever fears you are battling, take them to Jesus through the Word of God and combat them with the truth of God's Word. Jochebed covered that ark with prayer and walked many hours to see where God told her to place the ark. If this great woman had moved in fear, she would not have been able to even walk outside with a little ark containing her baby boy because the law prohibited it at the time.

Face your fears and be real with God. Talk to Him as you would a best friend. Jesus came so you could have life and have it more abundantly. (See John 10:10.) Quit living in your ability and live by the ability Jesus died to give you. The enemy loses his power over you when you become a child of God. Remember, God loves you and His love is protecting you.

Meditate on Colossians 2:14-15:

"Having wiped out the handwriting of requirements that was against us, which was contrary to us. And He has taken it out of the way, having nailed it to the cross. Having disarmed the principalities and powers, He made a public spectacle of them, triumphing over them in it."

Bow down on your knees and realize, God is waiting to release you from fear. He disarmed the enemy, Satan, and you need not be afraid. When this scripture says that the enemy has been disarmed, it means that the authority Satan had over your life has been ripped away from him. It is amazing to me to realize that I had nothing to do with my liberation from fear.

My dear sisters, just accept this gift and rest in Jesus through what the Word of God says about you. I love you and have already been praying over your freedom. Rest in faith and run from fear today.

Week 1, Day 3 — "What Did You Say, God?"

In looking at the Word of God and researching it, it is awesome to realize that whenever God uses the word "fear," it is often in the context of "Fear not" (also meaning "do not fear" or "do not be afraid"). This is an invitation to trust and rely upon God Almighty.

Let's look at Daniel 10:12. Here the angel of the Lord seeks to calm someone before speaking a divine revelation from God Almighty. My dear sisters, allow the Holy Spirit to calm you before you go any further with this revelation. God is pleading with you to trust Him and give Him all of your fears.

Over the past two days, are there any more fears you have discovered? If so, write them below:

_____

_____

Now, let's go back to Jochebed in Exodus 2. Can you imagine with me Moses becoming too loud for Jochebed to hide? She probably imagined hiding this beautiful child until he became a toddler and was too old to be considered a baby. Or perhaps Jochebed thought she would hide him until the Pharaoh's decree had passed. However, God Almighty wanted her to move out in faith and trust Him.

I see this with many women in our churches today. They are hiding their dreams and even their problems, thinking time will take care of everything. I remember being a little girl and thinking that if I reached a certain age, I would not be scared to go to sleep at night by myself. As a child, the night was such a scary time for me. I did not understand then why I had all of this anxiety and fear. As a six year old, I thought when I reached the teen years, these fears would just go away.

Recently, when I asked the Lord why this had been such a battle in my life, He revealed that most of the molestation I had been exposed to had happened during the night when everyone was asleep. Wow! What a revelation! Now I am believing God to completely heal this fear of the night and being afraid of being at home alone when my husband goes out of town on business trips. I refuse fear in the name of Jesus! (2 Timothy 1:7.)

My dear sisters, time will not heal these fears; only Jesus and His Word can do that. God is asking you to step out in faith and share what is bothering you the most. Let's take off our robes of fear with all of our dear sisters in Christ.

First Samuel 18:4 says, **"And Jonathan took off the robe that was on him and gave it to David, with his armor, even to his sword and his bow and his belt."** David and Jonathan were dear friends and loved each other deeply.

God can provide you with these kinds of sisters in Christ. First, let's take off our robes and make a covenant to pray for each other. Do not kid yourself, we are all hurting in one way or another. I was teaching a large group of women at a church with a membership of around two thousand, and it was amazing to learn of the pains they carried and never shared with anyone.

In the book of James, it tells us how to act with one another.

Write James 5:16 in the space below:

_____

_____

_____

Did you understand that it says you may be healed? Of course, I know Jesus is the Healer. However, many times He uses His people to be a sounding board. Listen to the needs of your sisters and bring them before the throne of our Father God. Be like Jonathan and remove your robes and your armor against sharing the truth of your life.

Recently, when I was in my ministry office writing this study, the Holy Spirit spoke to me and said: Jennifer, if anyone says he or she is making it while Jesus is absent from his or her life, it's only pretense. They are only faking it.

Isn't this liberating to know that many other women have fears just like you? Isn't it awesome to know that under the power of the Holy Spirit, you can be liberated as you take off the robe of fear? You are not supposed to be wearing this robe. Let us begin to take it off by first realizing it is there.

Now, back to Jochebed. Can you imagine the time when the Lord spoke to her spirit and told her to build an ark and to place it in the Nile River with her baby in it? She had to be moving in such faith. She had to realize that God was shutting the mouths of those crocodiles and causing them to look the other way.

The most amazing realization I felt when I was meditating on this story is that Jochebed knew Moses would be fine or she would never have sent Miriam to see what happened to him. Isn't it beautiful to know Miriam was preparing to see the providential hand of God Almighty?

What is the Nile crocodile in your life? Share what the enemy has been scaring you with recently or even all of your life:

_____

_____

_____

Many women tell me they are scared of their children becoming what they used to be before God delivered them. Or I hear women saying they never want to become what they saw their mothers or fathers become. There is so much fear in these statements. Do not connect yourself with fear anymore. Fear is a spirit and you will become what you focus upon in your life. Get away from fear of any kind. Focus on the Word of God and what God says you are.

Be honest with yourself and write down how you see yourself:

_____

_____

_____

Write out Psalm 45:11:

_____

_____

Incline your ears and hearts, my sisters, to the Lord Almighty. He sees you as His beautiful daughters and He is so proud of you in every way. All day today, say out loud: God thinks I am beautiful. Every time you have a negative thought of any kind, say out loud: God thinks I am beautiful. You see, as a person thinks in his own heart, so is he.

Write out Proverbs 23:7:

_____

_____

Jochebed had in her heart of hearts that her God would protect her baby boy. What is in your heart about God? Deep within many of our hearts is fear of not living up to God's expectations of us. We place on our Daddy in heaven the requirement placed upon us as children.

My dear sisters, the best dad in this world cannot compare with your Daddy in heaven. You are accepted and loved and He wants you to give Him all of your fears today. It is hard to believe that God wants our fears, but He does. Man wants our gifts and strengths, but God wants our fears and weaknesses. Give them to Him today and do not carry them yourself anymore.

Assignment:

Take a balloon and write all of your fears on it with a marker. Tomorrow morning send the balloon up to your Father in the sky. If you do not have time to do a balloon, write your fears on a sheet of paper. Then, take that paper and crumble it up and throw it away.

Do not carry those fears anymore. At this very moment, give them all to Jesus. He is standing at the right hand of God interceding on your behalf. I love you and know you will feel lightness in your step after finishing this assignment.

Meditate on Isaiah 60:15: **"Whereas you have been forsaken and hated, so that no one went through you, I will make you an eternal excellence."**

God will make you an eternal excellence. We all strive for excellence in many ways and to realize that God will do it is truly amazing. You are a daughter of the King, so step up to the Nile with your most treasured possession and know it is safe. Fear not. God is with you as you lay down your robe of fear.

Week 1, Day 4 — Beyond Your Wildest Dreams

As we are being delivered from the robe of fear, I want us to take a moment and dream a little. Would it not be great to live a life knowing your God will handle every situation that arises in your life beyond your wildest dreams? First, do not forget you have to be like Jochebed, totally devoted to Jesus.

Within our churches today, I see many people wanting all of the promises of God with great authority, but are not willing to pay the price to receive these promises. My sisters, "Do not receive condemnation with this statement."

Write out Romans 8:1:

_____

_____

_____

_____

You are always supposed to see the love of Christ, and conviction makes one get back in line with the Word of God. Condemnation makes one run and hide and feel unworthy to receive from God. When you are convicted, run to Jesus and ask, "What do I need to be doing now?" When He shows you where you can change or how you have sinned, live according to First John 1:9.

Write out 1 John 1:9:

_____

_____

Get clean and get back on the journey with the Lord of lords and the King of kings. He never left you. He just paused while you took a breather.

Okay, let's dream a little bit right here and remember that we serve a God for whom nothing is impossible! (Luke 1:37.) Bow your head and say out loud, "Father, in Jesus' name, show me a dream I have stopped dreaming due to fear. I received the dreams You placed within me as a little child. Let me dream again."

Write down your dream of dreams. Do not hold back. You are being delivered from fear.

Jochebed represents a woman who stood with unwavering faith and knew God Almighty could deliver her son. She was a believer and did not care what decree had been declared or what had happened to her neighbor's child. She placed Moses in the Nile and waited to see what God was going to do. Miriam stood back to see what was going to happen. Jochebed had trained her daughter in the things of the Lord. Scripture does not speak of either one as moving in fear or worry about Moses.

Suddenly, as the little ark floated among the bulrushes, the Pharaoh's daughter noticed it and sent one of her maids to retrieve it. Can't you just see Miriam waiting for this daughter of the most powerful man in the world to open the ark and see her beautiful baby brother? If Miriam had been afraid, she would have run home at this point. However, she stood by and waited to hear the response of the princess of Egypt. I'm sure she smiled to herself and thought, *Okay, brother, you are getting ready to go to the palace and Momma will be so proud.*

We see one of the most wonderful things happen as the princess of Egypt opened that little ark. She had compassion for the child. Miriam noticed this and asked if she needed a nurse to breast feed the baby. The princess was so overcome with love for this child that she told Miriam to go and find a nurse and she would gladly pay wages.

Read Exodus 2:9. When I read this passage, I wanted to jump up and down and scream, "God, You are awesome! The seed of the destroyer, Pharaoh, is paying your girl Jochebed to raise and nurse her own son."

My sisters, we have God in such a box with our puny prayers. Jochebed is our example. Step into the River Nile of your life and be willing to give it all up for Jesus. When He gives it back, you will be amazed.

What have you held on to and not handed over to God? Trust Him to even resurrect things you never thought possible. Move in faith and write down what you have been afraid to let go.

_____

_____

When I think of Jochebed rocking Baby Moses and nursing him, I know she made every minute count. We live in a society that does not embrace breast feeding as was practiced in biblical times. In the Old Testament, most mothers nursed their children until around age three. During this time, I know Jochebed told Moses how God saved his life and how he was marked for God's purposes.

My sisters, I feel just as convicted as I write about Jochebed teaching Moses. Many of us mothers do not have time with our children, so when we consider how busy our lives are, we should treasure every moment we can spend with them and tell them they are marked for God and that He has great plans for them.

Let us be like Jochebed with our mothering, marriages, single lives, and in our relations with other people in the world. Allow the Holy Spirit to show you whom you should be Jochebed to. Single women, there are so many children who are forgotten and need someone to believe in them. Mothers, do not take for granted those precious gifts God has given you. Take time to hug your children and impart to them the incredible teachings of our Lord and Savior Jesus Christ. Do not fret over your mistakes. We serve a God who can restore to you anything the enemy has stolen.

Write out Joel 2:25:

_____

_____

_____

_____

The enemy is a liar when he throws up in your face the awful mistakes you have made. Our God can take a mistake and make it into a miracle! I do not care what you have done. God can make it beautiful.

Relax and remember, it is not about you. Jesus is the glue that holds your life together. Personally, I know women who made so many mistakes they were placed in prison. They thought life was not worth living. However, when these women moved in faith, God gave them back their lives of freedom and restored their relationships. God's restoration is awesome! Move in faith for things you used to be afraid to believe.

Jesus loves you and is right now interceding at the right hand of God for your freedom from all fears. Give Him those nagging fears and know you can experience freedom beyond your wildest dreams.

Meditate all day on Ephesians 3:20 AMP:

"Now to Him Who, by (in consequence of) the [action of His] power that is at work within us, is able to [carry out His purpose and] do superabundantly, far over and above all that we [dare] ask or think [infinitely beyond our highest prayers, desires, thoughts, hopes, or dreams]."

Week 1, Day 5 — Freedom from Fear

Recently, as I sat in my ministry office, a beautiful brunette walked in to share her story. Her life had been destroyed due to alcoholism. She lost her two children, her marriage, and everything she owned. She had to start her life over and she was scared.

I talked with her and asked her where her Bible was. She replied that she was not quite sure. I told her she would never defeat the demon of alcoholism without grabbing onto the Word of God with both hands and feet and not ever letting go. If you had seen this woman on the streets, you would be amazed at how in control of her life she seemed to be, and you might even be a little bit envious of her good looks. This woman sat through service after service in a very large traditional church while her life was falling apart.

It is time for all of us Christians to get out of our boxes and daily ask the Lord who needs our help, but fear will keep us from doing that. God wants to release you from fear, because He desires that you be made whole so you can help others and the cycle can continue. Now, back to our lesson.

Write out Romans 8:15:

_____

_____

As you are being released from the bondage of fear, do not allow the enemy to take you back there. You have a promise in Romans 8:15 that you will not be in bondage again to fear. Believe it and receive it.

My sisters, whenever a fearful thought enters your mind, stand against it with the Word of God. Whenever I am battling a fear or a lie from the enemy, I answer the thought with a Bible verse.

Read Luke 4:1-13.

With what did Jesus answer all of the devil's temptations?

_____

_____

How do you answer the lies the devil throws at you about yourself or your family?

_____

_____

Let me give you a serious warning about reasoning or intellect. Do not try to reason your way around the enemy. When you go against him using the intellect, you are going to lose.

Second Corinthians 10:5 AMP states: **"[Inasmuch as we] refute arguments and theories and reasonings and every proud and lofty thing that sets itself up against the [true] knowledge of God; and we lead every thought and purpose away captive into the obedience of Christ (the Messiah, the Anointed One)."**

Do not go into the reasoning of your mind and think you can figure out every situation. God is much smarter than you and He has all of the answers in His Word. You are going to have to reprogram your mind to think like Jesus. Did you know the Word of God says we can have the mind of Christ? Yes, we can.

Write out 1 Corinthians 2:16:

_____

_____

Wow! My sisters, we can act and think like the Lord Jesus. How can we actually do this? The answer is to reprogram your way of thinking into what the Word of God says about you. Remember, I told you that John 1:14 says, **"The Word became flesh and dwelt among us."** Do you want more of the mind of Christ within you? Then, put more of the Word of God within you.

Be real today as we end this study on fear. Tell it to Jesus, as the old song says, and allow Him to carry your fears. You can be free from fear. My Jesus can do anything you need Him to do to allow you to live the abundant life He died to give you.

Write out your prayer in the space provided below and claim God's promises over your life. I am praying for you and I know you can be free to do all of the things you have dreamed of doing. Take off the robe of fear. It is an incredible feeling to be free of this robe.

One of the most powerful ways I daily combat the enemy is to say the entire Psalm 91 over me and my household. I place my family's name in the scripture to combat any lie the enemy would try to place in my mind. Try this for thirty days and watch fear dissipate from your life.

Write out a prayer to the Lord about taking off the robe of fear.

_____

_____

_____

_____

Meditate on the following scripture from Hebrews 10:23:

"Let us hold fast the confession of our hope without wavering, for He who promised is faithful."

Jesus took fear on the cross and you no longer have to wear that robe. Unbutton the buttons that have bound you for many years and fall into the arms of Jesus. You will never be the same. Live free and live for Jesus without the heavy robe of fear.

Week 2

Finally Letting Go of the Pain

Arise [from the depression and prostration in which circumstances have kept you—rise to a new life]! Shine (be radiant with the glory of the Lord), for your light has come, and the glory of the Lord has risen upon you!
Isaiah 60:1 AMP

A few years ago, sitting in my ministry office, I listened as a five-year-old boy described an act of molestation that he had experienced. It was a bright sunny day outside, but as this child described what had happened to him, it felt like a dark cloud had covered the sun. I asked the Holy Spirit to help me hold back the tears. I had not been told what the appointment was regarding, and the day outside did not fit the conversation I was hearing. As he shared about the moment at which the perpetrator demanded that he perform the perverted act, the child said one phrase that struck me and has never left my memory—and I quote him on this—"Mrs. Jennifer, it was like something dark went into my heart."

I knew what he meant.

This child's father had brought him to me for prayer because of my testimony of healing from sexual abuse. Children are so honest and genuine when they share their lives, and this child was especially intense. I will never forget his beautiful blue eyes piercing mine as he talked with me that day. And such spiritual depth! I was amazed that this precious little child was able to articulate with such clarity exactly what happens when a person is abused. Yes, something very dark enters that individual's life. For years I have said to multitudes all over the world—and I truly believe it—only Jesus can heal what abuse does to people.

It is absolutely heartbreaking to hear the many stories of helpless children who have experienced atrocities that only Satan himself could put in the hearts of man to commit. I once asked a professional counselor if the experts in the medical field had been able to determine what drives a grown man or woman to violate children in such vile ways. She admitted that they had not. To that I remarked, "I believe that Satan is the true instigator of these acts." This, of course, contradicts modern-day psychology, but the woman agreed that there is no other logical explanation.

After praying for this young child to be healed from the effects of what had been done to him, I could not help but think, *Oh, the blood of Jesus. It washes white as snow!* And I do thank God for that precious blood! I feel for the abused who do not know Jesus, for they cannot benefit from this cleansing flow. As a result they carry intense shame for the rest of their lives. How important it is for us to tell them about the Savior!

Next, I told the child how proud I was of him for telling his mommy and daddy what had been done to him. I assured him that he was a very smart and courageous boy not to keep secrets from his parents like the perpetrator had told him to do. Finally, this father and I walked his son through the steps to forgive the person who had harmed him. I adamantly assured the boy that what this person had done was wrong. I also explained that forgiving this man did not mean that we agreed with the evil behavior or excused it in any way. Evil is wrong. Period. I find it interesting that children often do not want their parents to tell the police. Despite being hurt and angry, they do not want to get the perpetrator "in trouble." But I am quick to explain that parents are obligated to inform the police in order to protect other children from being harmed by the person.

POINTING THEM TO THE WORD

I am neither a licensed therapist nor a professional counselor, and I am very careful not to overstep my bounds. In fact, I highly recommend Christian counseling. I am, however, a minister of the Gospel—the Good News—of Christ. For that reason and because of my testimony, children are often brought to me with the request that I pray for their healing. I consider it a privilege to pray over these precious ones, and I am confident that much restoration takes place.

I may not be qualified to offer professional, medical analysis and advice, but there is one thing I am qualified to do and I am faithful to do it: I always point these children and their families to the Word of God. Jesus is the only Savior, and His Word is the only source for true, ongoing healing. It alone can supply us with the power to "arise [from the depression and prostration]" caused by horrific circumstances. (See text verse, Isa. 60:1 AMP.) The apostle Paul called the Word the "sword of the Spirit," and it is just as powerful on our lips today as it was when Jesus defeated Satan's temptation. (See Eph. 6:17 and Matt. 4:1–11.)

LET THE LIGHT SHINE!

In Isaiah 60:1, the prophet speaks of a light that has come, and we are told to rise to a new life, to shine and be radiant with the glory of the Lord. Jesus, of course, is that light, and He even referred to Himself as "the light of the world" (John 8:12). When Jesus shines His light upon our darkness, we see more clearly and are able to rise to a new level of freedom. That is certainly good news for anyone groping in darkness as a result of abuse. The light of Jesus gives us hope that a new day has dawned as the twisted acts of Satan are finally exposed.

There is also another equally important aspect of the light. It reveals a second robe that Satan wants us to wear, the robe of unforgiveness. While unforgiveness and bitterness are certainly understandable—even justified as far as being a natural response to being victimized—it is a robe of darkness. In order for us to truly rise up victorious, every trace of darkness must be replaced by the light and love of Jesus. As long as there is unforgiveness, the one "wearing it" is forever linked to the perpetrator. Now this hardly seems fair, but true freedom can only exist where love reigns supreme. The elementary-

41

aged boy in my office that day had no problem forgiving the person who had wronged him, and I find this true for most children. Why, then, does it seem so difficult for us as adults? Jesus certainly understood this shortcoming and shared critical insight when He said, "Assuredly, I say to you, whoever does not receive the kingdom of God as a little child will by no means enter it" (Mark 10:15). We must become as little children and be quick to forgive.

It Will Help Make the Pain Go Away

When my children were very young, they occasionally suffered earaches. At times the pain became so intense that it actually caused them to scream. The pediatrician prescribed liquid antibiotics, which I was to give them orally, three times a day for fourteen days. Rebekah hated anything that tasted bad and when it was time for her to take the medicine, she would often say, "I don't like—yucky!" My response was always, "Honey, it will help make the pain go away." Then, after we prayed for healing, she would open her cute little mouth and swallow the pink liquid that was supposed to taste like bubble gum. When you convince children that bad-tasting medicine will relieve the pain, they usually cooperate.

When a person has suffered abuse, the pain can be excruciating. The Heavenly Father always responds to our cries for help, and along with His comforting words, He provides medicine that will help make our pain go away. The specific prescription for a person who has been victimized is forgiveness. As one who has had to forgive much, I adamantly agree that it does taste bad up front, but the healing that results yields glorious freedom from pain. The end result is so worth the difficult step to obey.

My sweet sister, with much understanding and compassion, I want to encourage you to take the medicine of the Word just like you would take a prescription to overcome an infection in your body. Unforgiveness and bitterness are as real as any physical cancer, and left to their own, they will eat away at your life until they totally destroy it. But they can be stopped! Regardless of how long you have carried the pain deep inside you, the Word of God is powerful enough to totally remove it. Hebrews 4:12 tells us that "the word of God is living and powerful, and sharper than any two-edged sword, piercing even to the division of soul and spirit, and of joints and marrow, and is a discerner of the thoughts and intents of the heart."

Many times I have run into women who thought they had forgiven their perpetrators, but once the light of the Holy Spirit through the Word of God shined on their hearts, they realized that there was still a measure of darkness needing to be dispelled. If that is the case with you, don't be discouraged. Remember, healing is a process, and God wants you to be whole, through and through. Whether the pain you are suffering is a result of abuse, divorce, or some other wrongdoing, no wound is too deep for Jesus to heal.

As I have stated, unforgiveness acts as a cancer, eating away at the person in its clutches, but its effects are not limited to the inner person.

We are triune beings—spirit; soul (mind, will, and emotions); and body—and what we carry in our hearts affects all areas of our lives. Physical ailments and even mental illness are often manifestations of deep-rooted issues. Of course, not all mental illness is a result of unforgiveness or abuse. A chemical imbalance in the brain can also wreak havoc in a person's life. The good news is, my sweet sister, Jesus can heal any sickness and His Word works. Let these words from the prophet Isaiah encourage you:

> **But He was wounded for our transgressions,**
> **He was bruised for our iniquities;**
> **The chastisement for our peace was upon Him,**
> **And by His stripes we are healed.**
>
> **Isaiah 53:5**

Today, let us shine the light of God's Word into the deep recesses of our souls and take our heavenly medicine. Let's forgive by the power of the Word of God, holding one another's hands tightly as we dare to be as children and forgive all who have wronged us. The apostle Paul said it this way:

> **Be gentle and forbearing with one another and, if one has a difference (a grievance or complaint) against another, readily pardoning each other; even as the Lord has [freely] forgiven you, so must you also [forgive].**
>
> **Colossians 3:13 AMP**

You may say, "But Jennifer, you don't know what this person did to me!"

And I say, "You're right. I do not know; but, I, too, have been wronged. And let me be real honest, *you cannot do this without the Holy Spirit!* But with Him, even forgiving your abuser is possible.

COMPLETELY FORGIVE

I will never forget one fall afternoon as I was preparing to minister in the local prison with a friend of mine. Because the weather was nice, I decided to take a walk outside to pray in a secluded spot on our property. Dave has always been supportive of my ministry and he was taking care of the children so I could be alone. Everything was fine as I began to pray, then—seemingly out of nowhere—the Holy Spirit spoke to my heart, *Jennifer it is time to completely forgive Joe.*

"What?" I was shocked. Hadn't I already done that? I was sure that I had.

Joe was an extended family member who repeatedly molested me for ten years and raped me when I was nine. Even though I honestly thought I had forgiven him, there was no denying that the Lord Jesus was directing me to do this now. The sickening feeling I was experiencing made it obvious that I was indeed holding unforgiveness toward the man who nearly destroyed my life. At one point, Ralph's abuse nearly drove me to put a gun to my head.

I screamed, "*How can I do that, Lord? It still hurts so bad!*" I knew that there was bitterness deep within me that needed to be removed. I dropped to the ground covered with fallen leaves, fell on my face, and pleaded for Jesus to help me because I knew I could not do it alone. Images of the abuse I suffered at Joe's hands flashed before me. The Lord revealed the intense hatred I felt toward this man for destroying my sexual boundaries. As a result of feeling worthless and used, I had given myself to many men before meeting the godly man I later married, my precious Dave. Although Dave never held my past against me, the Lord revealed that I was harboring bitter hatred and unforgiveness toward myself.

In addition to devastating effects that the sexual abuse had on me, I became terrified that my children might also fall prey to a predator. I had not been protected, so I became bound and determined to make sure Rebekah and David were kept safe, to the point that I was far too overprotective.

Now that the floodgates were opened, I realized that part of me was also still filled with rage toward my other tormentor, Scott, who had locked me in the corn silo so many times during my childhood. The affects of that torture carried over into my adulthood, affecting my ability to properly discipline my children. Oftentimes my pent-up anger toward him was misdirected toward my children, who became the recipients of my wrath. I was tormented by thoughts that someone—including myself—might hurt them. The guilt I experienced for subjecting my children to this out-of-proportion anger was immense. One thing I find over and over again from women who have been abused is that if the rage within them is not dealt with and removed, it will destroy the significant relationships in their lives. Oh, how I needed Jesus to help me!

And He did. As I poured out my heart and shed a torrent of tears, somehow I was finally able to let go—of Joe, Scott, and myself. As real as releasing a helium balloon on a windy day, I loosed my grip and let it all go. There are no words to describe the relief I experienced. The weight of the world had been lifted in a moment of time as the sweet freedom of forgiveness swept over me.

WHAT A DIFFERENCE!

As gut-wrenching as it was to forgive, something very definite changed in me. By the time I stopped crying, I *knew* that I was no longer a victim. Through the work of the Holy Spirit, a new Jennifer rose up "more than a conqueror" (Rom. 8:37), and I began praying with an authority I had never experienced before. It was a major turning point in my life, and I will never forget the prayer the Holy Spirit enabled me to pray:

Daddy God, in the name of Jesus, thank You for anointing me to speak to my sisters in prison tonight. I ask for many souls to be won for You and for many healings to take place as I go to minister freedom as never before. Daddy, thank You for Your anointing; and thank You for forgiving me as I forgive every person who has sinned against me! In Jesus' name.

Now, Satan, I address you! You ripped apart my childhood and adolescence. You nearly destroyed my children and my marriage. You almost succeeded in persuading me to take my own life, but you failed. I have obeyed my Father God by forgiving the people you have used against me. I have been washed clean by the blood of Jesus, and as the Word of God declares, I overcome you by the blood of the Lamb and the word of my testimony. (See Rev. 12:11.)

You are going to regret that you ever caused anyone to hurt me. Tonight I will minister under the anointing of the living God. In Jesus' name, I will tear down the strongholds of darkness that have held these women captive. With the help of the Holy Spirit, I will teach these women how to remove the ungodly robes they have worn as a result of things you have brought against them. I will snatch souls out of your kingdom and tell everyone in that place that the Lord Jesus has healed me and that He will heal them too. You are a defeated foe, in Jesus' name. Amen!

From that moment on, I began to walk in a boldness and authority that I had never known before. As a victim of abuse, I had cowered. But as a forgiven and healed child of God, I began to walk as an overcomer and conqueror in Christ. That evening at the prison was glorious as many women met the Lord and forgave their aggressors. They began to walk in the same freedom I had experienced that day in prayer.

FORGIVENESS AS A WAY OF LIFE

Over time, I learned that forgiveness is not just a one-time event. It is an integral part of what it means to be a Christian. Forgiveness is a way of life. What that means is that on a daily basis, I am quick to forgive any person who wrongs me and I refuse to fall for any demonic setup that would cause me to become offended. I have experienced firsthand the pain that unforgiveness causes, and I am not about to allow it back into my life by disobeying the Word of God or His command to forgive.

One thing I have come to realize is that the majority of people do not usually set out to hurt other people. The Lord made this clear to me one day when He reminded me of an encounter I once had with a very wounded dog. I so wanted to take the animal to the vet to be treated; however, every time I got close to the dog, it would growl. Several times it even made gestures as if it wanted to bite me. This animal was hurting and even though I wanted to help it, all it could do was lash out when I drew near. This speaks of an important principle we should never forget: "Hurting people hurt people."

When we come across wounded people, we should not be surprised or take it personally if they lash out. We are to simply obey the Word of God and forgive them. When we do, the door is opened for God to be our defense and to heal the pain in our lives. Today, take your spiritual medicine and obey these words of Jesus:

> **And whenever you stand praying, if you have any-thing against anyone, forgive him, that your Father in heaven may also forgive you your trespasses. But if you do not forgive, neither will your Father in heaven forgive your trespasses.**
>
> **Mark 11:25–26**

We have the best Daddy in the world, and if He says to do something, let us be determined to quickly obey like little children. When I took my "medicine" by throwing off the robe of unforgiveness that day, even though it tasted awful going down, it did indeed take away the pain. Will you come and be set free from your pain so you can enjoy the life God has given you?

This week in our study, you will learn how to recognize and remove that heavy, destructive robe of unforgiveness and replace it with the freedom of forgiveness. As you do, you will experience a new boldness and authority. Along with the apostle Paul, I am confident that you will be able to say, "I can do all things through Christ who strengthens me" (Phil. 4:13).

Week 2

Take Off the Robe of Unforgiveness

Week 2, Day 1 — Forgive Yourself — Part 1

Welcome to the second week of disrobing of things that should not be in a Christian's closet. Do not allow the "should not" in the previous sentence to bring condemnation upon you. We are looking at these robes together, and all of us have had to remove them.

Whenever I think I have missed the mark, I am reminded that the most powerful people in the Word often missed it. Think of King David. He missed it when he should have been at war with his people.

My dear sisters, this is a kind of war that we have entered to take back what the devil has stolen from our lives. Do not get sidetracked. Keep going into the second week in order to get rid of this most hideous robe that steals the joy of the Lord out of our lives.

Read 2 Samuel 11:1-4.

Where was King David supposed to be?

_____

_____

Where was King David? Why was he there?

_____

_____

King David, as we know from the above verses, stayed in Jerusalem when he was supposed to go out to battle. Think with me a little. If you have time, look back at Second Samuel 10 and you will see that King David had just been to war earlier and led a great victory against the Ammonites and Syrians.

I know you just had a victory last week, and we need to conquer an even bigger battle this week — one that will bring freedom. So don't stay in the comforts of Jerusalem. It is just a setup of the enemy.

You see, this is how unforgiveness is in many cases. It is so much more comfortable to stay away from those who have hurt us. It is more comfortable not to confront issues that are stealing the very faith we need to conquer the issues in our lives. If you have any unforgiveness in your life, your faith channel to God is full of static and you cannot hear from your Daddy in heaven as you will be able to after disrobing.

In your own words, what does it mean to you to forgive?

_____

_____

According to *New Webster's Dictionary and Thesaurus*, the definition of the word "forgive" is: (1) to pardon; to cease to bear resentment against; to cancel (as a debt).[2]

One thing I find repeatedly wrong with the women of the Body of Christ that I do not see discussed often is that women have a hard time forgiving themselves. I vividly saw this exemplified recently while at a luncheon with some dear friends. We were eating when the cell phone of one of the women rang. I heard her invite someone to stop by the restaurant. Little did I know it was a woman I had prayed for on the phone a few days earlier. At that time, a physical miracle happened and she was delivered from a sickness that she had had for many years.

When she showed up, she was glad to see me in person and we hugged. I could tell she was weary and through another one of the women talking and praying for her, the Holy Spirit told me she was carrying unforgiveness towards herself about motherhood. When I spoke this to her, she wept. I said another prayer for her and saw this invisible yoke taken off of her life. She had not been walking with the Lord for too many years and had made mistakes with her first child.

My dear sisters, learn to forgive yourselves. Remember, Jesus is the glue that keeps your life together. You are not held together by your own efforts. Today women are having to wear too many hats and it's impossible to be everything to everybody. Rest in the Lord.

Read John 15:1-5.

Who is the vinedresser?

_____

_____

Who is the One who prunes the vines to bear more fruit?

_____

_____

You cannot forgive yourself or others without the help of the Holy Spirit. Remember the phrase, "Hurting people hurt people"? People are not out there trying to offend you so you'll carry this heavy robe of unforgiveness. Many dear women are carrying the weight of not living up to this imaginary line of perfection which no one can attain. Rest in the Lord. Love yourself. The most important Person in the entire universe loves you and wants you to forgive yourself.

[2]*New Webster's Dictionary and Thesaurus* (New York, NY: Ottenheimer Publishers, Inc., 1991), 158.

Let me end today's lesson with a personal thing I had a very hard time forgiving myself for. At the age of thirty, my life fell apart. It was a terrifying time for me. I entered the world of clinical depression and I did things I was so ashamed of that I would not make them known to my counselor. I tried to be the perfect Mom, because I never really felt loved as a child. I had a toddler and a baby and was literally losing my mind. There were days when I would have rages and did not know what was happening to me. There were days I was anything but the great Mom I was trying to be.

Finally, the Holy Spirit said to me, "Jennifer, you talk with many women and constantly tell them there isn't anything Jesus can't forgive them for. Now, go with Me and let's teach you to forgive yourself."

When the Lord took me back and said, "There is not any sin I cannot forgive except to blaspheme the Holy Spirit," I started seeing how I had abused myself. Jesus had already forgiven me ten years earlier when I cried out in desperation, asking Him to come into my life and deliver me. However, I did not forgive myself.

When I forgave myself, I felt like a little girl running into the arms of my Daddy, knowing all of my sins and mistakes were covered by the blood of Jesus. The relief I felt cannot be described.

Please allow yourself this forgiveness. I do not care what you have done. I have counseled women who have rejected their children because of past drug abuse and women who have aborted babies. Jesus forgave them and all is erased from their past.

Forgive yourself and say over and over again all day long, "Jesus died for my forgiveness and I am loved!"

Meditate on Proverbs 3:3-6:

"Let not mercy and truth forsake you; bind them around your neck, write them on the tablet of your heart,

"And so find favor and high esteem in the sight of God and man.

"Trust in the Lord with all your heart, and lean not on your own understanding;

"In all your ways acknowledge Him, and He shall direct your paths."

Today is your day to walk down the road of forgiving yourself. I love you, my dear sisters, and I wish I could hug you in person. However, the Lord Himself is walking with you. Lean on Him, not on your own understanding.

We will unbutton more buttons tomorrow. Again I say to you, my dear sisters, rest in the Lord.

Week 2, Day 2 — Forgive Yourself — Part 2

Yesterday was a necessary day in the disrobing of unforgiveness. However, I am sure you can tell by the title of today's study that we are not finished with forgiving ourselves. The Holy Spirit would not let me leave this topic, and I cannot begin to abandon His guidance in writing this Bible study.

Whenever we forgive ourselves, we see ourselves in a new light. Whenever we see ourselves as Jesus sees us, we can live the lives He died on Calvary to give to us. Let's head down this final lane together to make sure we have truly forgiven ourselves.

Last week, a partner with my ministry called and asked me to go visit her son, a crack addict. When we sat at his kitchen table talking, all I could think of was that this man had not forgiven himself for all the years of drug use. He could not even begin to forgive himself for losing his marriage, his children, and the respect of people in his community. He just wept and wept and said what a sorry person he was.

As an outsider looking in on a situation, it is easy to say, "Forgive yourself so you can stop this destructive behavior." However, we all have destructive behavior that is due to unforgiveness. My destructive behavior was alcohol and cigarettes. Then, when those pitfalls were eliminated, there was eating, shopping, etc. Not until I truly forgave myself for all of my mistakes did I start living the abundant life. I would forgive people for anything and still be down on myself for not living up to the perfectionist standards that absolutely no human could attain.

Ask the Holy Spirit to show you areas you have never forgiven yourself for. Then, write them in the space that follows:

_____

_____

_____

_____

Read 2 Samuel 9:1-13.

Where did Mephibosheth live?

_____

Lo-debar means "a thing of nought." This was a place of nothing. Here we have the grandson of a past king of Israel living in total poverty. When King David called him forward to bless him in keeping with an agreement he had with Jonathan, his father, what did this man in the line of loyalty call himself?

How do you see yourself? Pay attention today to the tape recording in your mind about yourself. Look up Titus 3:2. You are not to slander anyone, including yourself. This verse also says that we are to be courteous to everyone, again including ourselves. Jesus paid a high price for you and He wants you to walk in this life of abundance.

How we see ourselves affects everything around us and inside of us. We treat ourselves in the way we see ourselves. When you have forgiven yourself, you can truly forgive others, according to the Lord's wishes. It may not be easy for others to see that you have not forgiven yourself, but you know yourself the areas that seem to torment you.

Right now, bow your head and say out loud the things that have tormented you over the years. First Peter 5:7 says, **"Casting all your care upon Him, for He cares for you."** It is time to cast those cares over and do not receive them back again. Even though I am sure many of you have asked the Lord to forgive you for your past sins, it is time now to forgive yourself.

Make this confession out loud: *I forgive myself in the name of Jesus and refuse to carry these burdens any longer. I am forgiven and will walk in this freedom today. I love You, Lord Jesus, and receive Your forgiveness totally for past sins and mistakes. In Jesus' name I pray. Amen.*

Write down how you feel after praying this prayer:

_____

_____

Write out Ephesians 2:5-6:

_____

_____

_____

Write out Isaiah 41:10:

_____

_____

Write out Jeremiah 31:3-4:

_____

_____

_____

_____

The Lord loves you, my sisters in Christ, and He is glad to send an attendant to receive this robe of unforgiveness. Be free and look at the sunshine and flowers again as a little child would. Run through the meadows and know your Daddy in heaven is watching over your every step.

Remember John 8:36 AMP: **"So if the Son liberates you [makes you free men], then you are really and unquestionably free."** Hallelujah! You are free from this heavy robe of unforgiveness! Be blessed as you set out for your day and remember, according to Deuteronomy 28:2, blessings are chasing you down!

Week 2, Day 3 — Forgiveness Is Tough but So Worth It!

The robe of unforgiveness can take many forms in our lives. However, we need to take it off for many reasons. The most prominent reason we need to forgive is that Jesus commanded us to do this. Today let's become full of the Word so we can see we are not just forgiving people because we know it's the right thing to do.

The Senior Pastor at my church preached a sermon one Sunday that really has stayed with me. He said, "We may know something, but our actions prove what we believe." Today I want the Word of God to convince you, my sisters, that forgiveness is not optional. When you truly believe it is God's will for you to forgive every offense, you will take off a robe and live a true life of quality.

One of my dear sisters in Christ is a counselor with a thriving practice in my hometown. I asked her if unforgiveness could cause mental illness, and she said, "Most definitely." Many forms of mental illness are caused by not forgiving a person and allowing that unforgiveness to turn into bitterness. Many marriages fall apart due to holding grudges and never discussing the offense.

Over the last few years, I have learned to try to do daily maintenance to make sure I have no unforgiveness in my life. You cannot move the mountains out of your life if you have not forgiven your brother or sister or a stranger who woke up on the wrong side of the bed. When I first started this maintenance of cleansing myself of unforgiveness, it was an unusual affair. However, now if I am not feeling like myself, I make sure I am not holding grudges or unforgiveness in my heart toward anyone.

Write out Mark 11:23-26:

_____

_____

_____

_____

I have always used Mark 11:23 when I preach about faith. However, the Holy Spirit had me read through verses 25 and 26 and I was shocked. Is it true I cannot really move in faith when I have a grudge against someone? Isn't it amazing how we rationalize things? There is nothing we can use as an excuse for not forgiving someone. You may say, "But you do not know how I have suffered." What is amazing is that you truly do not know how bad others have suffered in their lives, yet you forgave their offenders.

Recently in a conference, I was able to counsel a beautiful woman whom I could see during our prayer sessions at the altar was not getting the breakthrough she needed. The Holy Spirit kept bringing me back to her when I preached and in between the sessions.

Finally, I asked the Lord what to do. He told me to take her aside along with the Pastor of the church and speak with her. While we were talking to her, she related how she had suffered as a small child by the hands of her mother in ways too horrible to write about. After prayer she wept and we led her to forgive her mother.

Now, my sisters, this was not a small matter because while she was talking to us, I cried and remembered thinking this was the most horrible story I had heard so far in my ministry. We think we are really doing something when we find out a best friend has betrayed us. Isn't it amazing how God really opens our eyes when we ask Him to?

I ran into a friend I used to attend church with and felt the tension caused by the awareness of negative comments he had made about my ministry. I had to come home and do some maintenance on my forgiveness and realized that the way I felt when I saw him suggested I had not completely forgiven him. Be honest with yourself today. Remember, those people we were closest to sometimes are the hardest to forgive.

Make a list of the people in your life that you honestly know you have not forgiven. (This list may grow as the Holy Spirit deals with your heart.)

_____

_____

_____

_____

Write out Matthew 6:12:

_____

_____

Do you have any debts to the Lord? Are there areas in your life you need help with on a daily basis? The Apostle Paul said he had not yet attained, so let us not kid ourselves. We need some mercy also. Go ahead and be honest. We all need forgiveness. Therefore, we need to forgive other people. Galatians 6:7 says, **"Whatever a man** [woman] sows, that he [she] **will also reap."** I desire to sow forgiveness because I know I will need forgiveness from others.

Write a prayer asking the Lord to start preparing your heart to forgive those offenses you have lodged deep within your heart:

_____

_____

_____

_____

_____

Remember, the Lord loves you and wants you free to be all you can be. When I started letting the Lord deal with me about unforgiveness, it was a painful process. In America, we just want the good and beautiful experiences. However, my dear sisters, we all fall short of the glory of God. (Romans 3:23.)

Remember, we are forgiven by the blood of Jesus, not by our deeds. The Lord wants us to forgive others so we can be free. How about not carrying those feelings toward people anymore? How about being free of all of your own condemnation of knowing you should forgive but not having done so? Remember, you cannot do it alone! Jesus went back to heaven to send the Holy Spirit to be our Helper and Comforter. Allow Him to help you today to be free and liberated from the bondage of unforgiveness toward others.

Make a list of people you have tried for years to forgive but haven't been able to. Some of those people may be within your own families and homes.

_____

_____

_____

_____

Leave those names in the hands of the Lord Jesus Himself. We will deal with them again tomorrow. You are my family in the Lord and I love you.

Have an incredible day and know you have been obedient thus far. Pat yourself on the back and rejoice that you have made it this far. Traveling this narrow road is so worth the final destination. You are beautiful to your Daddy as you take your first baby steps to be freed from your robe of unforgiveness. He holds your hand and will not let you go until He knows you will not fall down. Be free and meditate on the following verses once again:

Psalm 45:10-11 AMP — **"Hear, O daughter, consider, submit, and consent to my instruction: forget also your own people and your father's house;**

"So will the King desire your beauty: because He is your Lord, be submissive and reverence and honor Him."

You are beautiful to the King of kings and the Lord of lords. Many days I used to feel so incredibly unattractive and wanted to hide from everyone. Oh, my dear sisters, you are all so beautiful and the Lord desires to show you off to the world. Be at peace and know you are loved by someone who will NEVER stop loving you. NEVER! Rest in His arms and enjoy the journey to getting a new wardrobe.

Week 2, Day 4 — Forgiveness Freely Given

As a believer in Christ, forgiving others is the basis of our relationship with Him. We truly cannot move into an intimate relationship with the Lord until we learn to be like Jesus. I notice sometimes the hardest people to forgive are those within our own house. Now, many of you think I mean the "house" of those in your biological family. However, I mean those in the family of God.

Read Matthew 12:46-49.

In your own words, sum up what is taking place in these verses:

_____

_____

_____

Do you realize what boundaries there are for the Lord to consider people to be His family? We have to do the will of the Father in heaven. Now, again let's look at Matthew 6:12. When we read that our forgiveness in Christ is dependent upon how we forgive others, it truly gives us a different perspective on our need to forgive. When we truly think of all the Lord has forgiven us, then we start waking up to reality.

Listen closely, my sisters. If it were not for the grace of God, where would we be? We have all fallen short of the glory of God according to Romans 3:23. Did you hear the "all" in this verse? Let me say this again: We have all fallen short of the glory of God. The glory of God means living a life that glorifies the Lord Jesus.

People are always saying to me that I have such a gift of mercy towards people. I cannot help but have this gift because I know all I was forgiven of by Jesus. We all should have a gift of mercy. If it were not for Christ dying on the cross over two thousand years ago, absolutely none of us could stand in the presence of a holy God.

Write out Ephesians 2:4-5:

_____

_____

_____

_____

Did you hear that it was by the grace of God that you were saved? You did not impress God with your educational background or family heritage. You did not impress God with your charity work or membership in civic clubs. It is by the grace of God you have been saved. We speak a great deal about grace within the church today.

Grace is defined by many biblical scholars as the unmerited favor of God. We can do nothing to earn the love and adoration of God. We received the most incredible gift in the world when we accepted Jesus in our hearts. Think about it. We did not do anything to earn this grace, and we do not have to perform to keep the grace of God in our lives.

When you fall in love with Jesus, you desire to please Him just as you did when you fell in love for the first time with a fellow human. When I was dating my husband, I just could not do enough to please him. Dave was a bachelor living alone. I would clean his house to surprise him and do all of his laundry. As I was cleaning, I would get so excited about him coming home and finding his house clean and calling me to say thanks for doing such a loving thing. I could not wait for his phone call.

When I moved into his house after marriage, cleaning did not feel as exciting (wink!). Now I do not do these things so Dave will love me more. It is my heart pouring out to him and the children, letting them know they are loved and taken care of.

Now, back to the grace of God. I feel I could never judge anyone for the lives they are leading in sin. All I want to do is tell them Jesus loves them and that He can make it all right. If it had not been for the grace of God, I know I would be in jail or in the grave. I spent a childhood being abused. A member of my extended family began sexually molesting me from about age four to the age of fourteen. There are no pleasant memories of my childhood, because most of my memory is wiped out by these incidents of abuse. I do not have memories of a wonderful home with a sense of security and safety. My memories would bring tears to your eyes and nightmares would plague you.

I share this to say that whenever I read a statistic about prostitution in America, I have to drop my head and cry. It is a proven fact that when you look into the background of prostitutes, in nearly every case you will find sexual abuse. I realize that except for the grace of God, I could be walking the streets of America and selling my body for financial gain. Therefore, how could I ever look down on anyone for what the devil has trapped them into doing? The main thing I need to do as a believer is to say, "Come and hear about the love of God."

Recently, I had the opportunity to speak into the life of a prostitute in our area. My ministry had provided her children with school clothes and supplies. As I dropped off the children's clothes, I looked directly at this woman and told her Jesus loved her. I remember her hollow stare as she stood there seeming to say, "You just do not understand my life." I hugged her and told her I loved her and would pray for her.

I wish I had a happy ending to this story, but I do not. Her children have been removed and are living in an orphanage. As I heard of this situation which I spent years working on, I lay in bed weeping. My husband held me and said, "Jennifer, you did all you could." He was so sweet to be concerned about his wife, but my tears were for the fact that had it not been for the grace of God, there I could be also.

I was relieved that these sweet children had finally been removed from that awful environment. However, I could not get away from the necessity to show love and tell people Jesus loves them, even if in my flesh I want to scream at them.

Remember, you were once in your sins, and without Jesus you could once again be in the same boat. I don't mean to say you are in any way to condone the lifestyles of the world. Believe me, this woman knew the life she was living was wrong because she always seemed anxious when I came into the driveway. All I could do was tell her Jesus could make her whole and she did not have to live her life that way. The last I heard she had been arrested for child prostitution and is now awaiting trial.

Right now all I can think of is John 10:10. The enemy has stolen once again and we, as believers, have to be equipped with forgiveness in our hearts so he cannot steal from us as well.

Returning to the initial scripture in this lesson, Matthew 12:46-49, we have to do the will of God to be in the family of God. Repent of any unforgiveness and take off any ugly robe you are wearing. We all want to be in the family of God, and we are if we have made Jesus the Lord of our lives.

Let go of those bad feelings and grudges and live in freedom. Your Daddy is holding your replacement robe now, which is the forgiveness He died to be able to place upon your person. You will enter into an intimate relationship with Him as you obey His Word and allow Him to take off that ugly robe that has stolen your joy.

I love you, my sisters, and say, "Hang in there with me." We are almost ready to leave this dressing room of unforgiveness. Remember, you're only free to love when you have forgiven others.

Write out Ephesians 2:13:

_____

_____

Write out Ephesians 3:17-19:

_____

_____

_____

_____

_____

_____

Write out 1 John 4:16:

_____

_____

Be at peace, my sweet sisters in the Lord. We are family and I refuse to allow any unforgiveness to separate me from you. However, most importantly, I refuse to allow any unforgiveness to make it impossible for me to have the relationship I have with my Daddy in heaven. Join in with me, bow your heads, and forgive all of those who have wronged you so you can be free today.

Tomorrow we will remove this robe of unforgiveness. Remember, you can do all things through Jesus who gives you strength. (Philippians 4:13.)

Week 2, Day 5 — Yes, You Can Be Free!

For the second morning in a row, I joined my husband Dave in the gym. This is a big deal for him, because he is such a disciplined man. He wants us to work out together, not only so we can be healthy, but so we can spend time together early in the morning.

Now, let me be honest. Getting up at 5:30 a.m. and walking on the elliptical trainer and lifting weights is anything but fun for me. However, when my husband took me shopping recently and I could not button my usual size, I realized there was a problem and there was some significance to what Dave had been telling me about working out together to stay in shape.

I wanted to scream in that dressing room when I realized I had gained weight. Dave had taken me out to buy clothes for me to preach in and I could not get the button or the zipper to fasten. Dave had the money in hand, but I had to face the reality that I could not receive his gifts because I had outgrown the size I always told myself I would never exceed.

Now, why do I share this story with you? Our heavenly Father has many gifts to offer us: peace and joy, for example. However, we cannot truly accept them until we obey the Word of God and become free. We may think we are doing all right just as I did until I had to face reality in that dressing room.

If you are not living the abundant life Jesus promised in John 10:10, then you may have some shedding of unforgiveness pounds to do or you will not fit into the clothes your Daddy has already bought for you. Get those weights of the Word in your hand and use them. Walk in faith, knowing you can obey the Word and truly live in the shadow of the Almighty. (Psalm 91.)

Now, let's move on to the final day of dealing with unforgiveness.

Write out Ephesians 4:30-32:

_____

_____

_____

_____

_____

Write out Ephesians 5:1-2:

_____

_____

_____

_____

Whom are you supposed to be imitating in the way you live your life?

_____

_____

It is a high call to be imitators of the Lord Jesus. This truly says that when others wrong us, we are to forgive. Once again, I do not say that we are to be doormats and live with a "victim" mentality, allowing ourselves to be abused in the name of forgiving others. We are to remove ourselves and our children if there is abuse. I have spoken to many women and have told them that they should absolutely not allow their children to stay in the same house with their dad if he is a pedophile. Use wisdom as the Lord says in His Word.

Get counseling, go to your pastor, and allow the Holy Spirit to show you the path through the Word of God. Our heavenly Father would never want His girls and His precious children to endure abuse. However, we have to forgive with the help of the Holy Spirit, and to be truly honest, we cannot forgive without the Holy Spirit.

Right now, say this prayer with me:

Father, in Jesus' name, I ask You to anoint me to forgive _____ for all the years of _____. Dear Jesus, I cannot do this on my own. I ask You to wash me clean and let me feel Your arms around me as I take this step of faith. Thank You for helping me and loving me as Your child, in Jesus' name. Amen.

I remember standing behind my house and staring out over the marsh, asking the Lord how He could allow all the years of abuse to happen in my life. I felt it was impossible to forgive the man who molested me, raped me at age nine, stole my childhood, and almost stole my life as I contemplated taking the step to suicide.

The Lord answered me that all that sin originated in the Garden of Eden with the serpent. Then He walked me through the healing and forgiveness.

Many years ago, as I wept in the arms of the Lord, I felt as if I'd realized His call upon my life. That specific evening, I was going to the local prison to share my testimony with some women inmates. As I felt the Lord enabling me to forgive this man, I remember saying out loud, Devil, you may have stolen my childhood and almost stolen my life, but tonight I am going to rip up your kingdom of darkness in the name of Jesus! I am going to share under the anointing of my Daddy how Jesus made me whole and how these women can become whole too.

Praise God! That night I shared my testimony and I saw women weep and ask Jesus to make them whole. The enemy may be trying to destroy you through the abuse you have experienced and even through the abuse you have placed upon others. However, allow your Daddy to show you how He can take all of your pain and turn it into a testimony for the glory of God.

Many times I have seen women who used to be prostitutes weep and accept the love of the Lord and forgive others and themselves.

At a Pennsylvania conference I held a few years ago, I met a precious woman who had lived a life of prostitution and crack addiction. You cannot imagine how beautiful it is now to see her sharing her story with women who are hurting with the same past of addiction. She is so full of forgiveness for others and just loves the women the Lord places in her path. Being used in this manner means she has walked down the path of forgiveness. There were many abusers in her life and rejection from her family, but she walks in the glory of the Lord because she has forgiven and accepted the forgiveness of her Daddy in heaven.

Read Matthew 16:24-26.

What does taking up the cross mean in your life today?

_____

_____

_____

_____

How can forgiving others be like taking up the cross?

_____

_____

_____

_____

Die to yourselves, my sisters, and receive the love and acceptance of the Lord. Get rid of this robe and receive the robe of knowing you are covered by your Father in heaven. As a little girl, whenever someone did something wrong to you, you would run to your daddy and tell him all about it. Now, your Daddy in heaven will handle the outcome of the wrongs done to you. In other words, when we truly forgive, then the outcome of our situations is in the hands of our loving Father. Walk in faith and obey the Word of God no matter what.

I sense you are ready to receive the beautiful robe of forgiveness and walk much more confidently today as you know the Lord has taken off this ugly robe and replaced it with His beautiful robe that gloriously fits you. I love new clothes. However, my spiritual clothes are what make me glow and assure me that things are going to be all right.

Accept this robe and share with your sisters in Christ how it finally feels to be rid of all unforgiveness. I love you and look forward to next week as we remove yet another robe to get dressed in another beautiful piece of clothing given us by our Daddy in heaven.

Meditate on this verse: **"I will be a Father to you, and you shall be My sons and daughters, says the Lord Almighty"** (2 Corinthians 6:18). Receive this verse and accept that you are a child of the King and are loved for all eternity.

No More Rules

[Jesus said,] "You did not choose Me, but I chose you."
John 15:16

There are many rules one has to learn in life and not all of them are bad. In fact, some are very necessary for living an orderly life. It is also important to submit to the proper authorities; otherwise anarchy would result. There are, however, abuses of authority as well as religious rules that hold people in bondage. These I disdain, because I was subjected to them from a very young age and suffered from their effects for many, many years. I call these religious rules a "robe of religion and tradition," and its supposed purpose is to make women "good enough" to be loved and accepted by God.

I began learning rules very early, primarily because my family belonged to an extremely legalistic religious group, which I now know is a religious cult. There were rules about what to wear and which hairstyles were acceptable. We were even told what our opinions should be toward others, based on how well or how poorly they followed the rules. To make matters worse, the whole system was confusing because the members within the group debated over the rules, which in turn caused division and strife. The atmosphere was anything but peaceful as these adults could not even agree on how long a woman's shirt sleeve had to be in order for her to be acceptable to God.

After enough years of this, I found myself just pretending to follow the rules and then secretly slipping into my purse the clothes that I liked to wear. I knew I had to be careful because the repercussion of being caught breaking the rules within the system was condemnation so severe that it was unbearable. I surely did not need that because the condemnation I heaped upon myself was already choking the life out of me. When I wore shorts or a bathing suit, I was convinced that the Lord was upset with me and would not even hear my prayers if I called upon Him.

It is sad because although I heard about Jesus throughout my childhood, He was portrayed as rigid and difficult to please. He was certainly not a healer. Trying to please Him, my life became an endless cycle of striving and failure. As long as I could live up to the rules, I could feel loved in the presence of God; but if I had a bad day of "rule breaking," I was convinced that He did not love me anymore. Then I'd start over, trying to please God by following the multitude of rules again, but no matter how hard I tried, I never could manage to do it. Finally, when it became clear that I could not attain the standard, I gave up and joined the world full force. Leaving home for college at the University of North Carolina in Chapel Hill provided the perfect opportunity to break free of the tyranny.

A RAY OF HOPE

As you can imagine, swinging the other direction and living a worldly lifestyle hardly provided the peace and acceptance I was searching for. But then came a break in the clouds. I met the two people who would become my spiritual parents, Reverend and Mrs. Roy Belon. With open arms they welcomed me into their fold and for two years I had the privilege of sitting under their ministry. They introduced me to a God I had never heard of before. I was amazed because this God did not have a long list of do's and don'ts, and I found that He was loving and gentle.

My heart wanted to believe, but because my former religious indoctrination was so deeply ingrained, part of me would not totally surrender to the Belon's God or the Jesus they knew. How could He really be as understanding as they portrayed Him? And to think that He didn't have a list of rules! How could that be? To hear the Belons say that He was offering me salvation as a *free gift* was almost impossible to fathom. Nevertheless the words of the following verse began to penetrate my heart:

> **For it is by free grace (God's unmerited favor) that you are saved (delivered from judgment and made partakers of Christ's salvation) through [your] faith. And this [salvation] is not of yourselves [of your own doing, it came not through your own striving], but it is the gift of God.**
>
> **Ephesians 2:8 AMP**

THE DEVIL COMES IMMEDIATELY ...

I wish I could say that after that, it was smooth sailing and I lived happily ever after. But that is not very realistic. Jesus even warned that when the Word is sown in the hearts of people, "Satan comes at once to try to make them forget it" (Mark 4:15 TLB). His assault began with a phone call from my biological parents.

After working for a company in my hometown for nearly thirty years, my father lost his job just weeks before he had planned to retire. With no warning, the entire plant was shut down, which came as a great shock. To further add insult to injury, the company notified my dad that they would not honor his retirement! With three of the children in our family away at college, the news could not have come at a worse time. For my sister and me, this meant that we had to move back home to finish our education at the University of North Carolina at Wilmington. My older brother was on full scholarship to Wake Forest University, so his plans did not change.

Leaving my college life and my new spiritual parents was devastating. I felt like I moving back to hell itself. The Belons reassured me that I was not going alone—that God would take care of me. I embraced their words, but I knew it was going to be extremely difficult to go back into that restrictive religious system. I had become accustomed to my new lifestyle at college and had broken many of the "family rules." Now

63

I was going to have to face that strict God and His endless set of rules again. After having been introduced to a God of joy, I dreaded having to be subjected to the condemning sermons from the minister I had grown up listening to.

HERE WE GO AGAIN

Buoyed by my newfound faith and the prayers of my new spiritual parents, I braced myself and headed home. I found that little had changed—except for me. And I had changed more than I realized. Although I did not voice it audibly, I found myself asking, *Where did all of these rules come from? And who decided that we had to work ourselves up to God?* It wasn't long, however, before the questions went by the wayside and I was caught up in the system all over again. I was not yet strong enough to withstand the constant bombardment of legalism that permeated the atmosphere. Rules, rules, and more rules garnered my life.

Even in the midst of this oppression, however, God was watching over me. A few years after returning home, I met and married Dave Kostyal, one of the most godly men I have ever known. To this day, he is truly my knight in shining armor. Dave had grown up Catholic, but out of love for me, joined the religious system of my youth. Literally laying down his life for me, Dave did everything a man could possibly do to love and support me, but the downward spiral that had overtaken me was out of control.

Depression and despair were my only reward as I continued wearing the robe of religion and tradition in an effort to please God. To further contribute to the all-out satanic assault, day and night I became tormented by flashbacks of the abuse I had suffered as a child. Terrified that something might happen to my young children, the mental oppression and fatigue reached the point that I could not even remember my name, much less all the rules I was supposed to keep up with.

Finally, at age thirty-one, everything came to a head. Extreme exhaustion had devoured me both physically and emotionally, and in my mind I only had two options—suicide or check into a mental hospital. Unable to find our gun, I finally collapsed onto the living room floor where Dave found me in a heap.

LIGHT IN THE DARKNESS

Lest you think that this crisis was the beginning of the end, let me assure you, the only end was an end to the life of torment I had led. What Satan no doubt thought was his crowning blow to snuff me out was actually the beginning of an entirely new life, a new life of freedom that I did not even know was possible.

There on that living room floor, in utter despair, I cried out for Jesus to reveal Himself to me. Dave, too, cried out to God, "Lord, have mercy on my wife! She cannot go on like this anymore."

And mercy did come. In the midst of my darkness, Jesus shined His glorious light and began to reveal Himself to me in a new way. Our cries had gotten heaven's attention, and immediately circumstances were set into motion and people were mobilized to come to our aid. My housekeeper told me about her sister who had been healed of sexual abuse through the Lord Jesus, and this opened a door for the Holy Spirit to work. Within two weeks I was radically saved and filled with the Holy Spirit. After years of an agonizing search, I finally met *Jesus*—the Prince of Peace. And these weren't just familiar words that I had heard from the Bible. I came to know Him *personally*—as *my* Prince of Peace. When I finally saw Him as He really is, I fell head over heels in love with Him, and I have never been the same.

NOTHING NEW UNDER THE SUN

Most likely you did not grow up under the extreme religious legalism that I did; however, my guess is that you do find yourself constantly trying to please God in order to be acceptable to Him. Perhaps it stems from trying to please a parent who—no matter how hard you tried—withheld his or her approval. Even if the root cause is different or if the legalism is much more subtle in your life, let me assure you that Satan is behind every form of pressure that drives you to perform. This robe of religion and tradition may appear to be godly, but it is designed to keep you from experiencing true freedom in Christ. Its purpose is to trick you into believing that if you will just try a little harder, then you will be acceptable, then you will be good enough to be loved. But it is a demonic deception designed to keep you on an endless treadmill until you simply lose heart and give up.

Let's see what the Bible has to say about this robe. If anyone knew about rules and tried to keep them, it was the apostle Paul. In his letter to the Philippian church, he wrote:

> **I have more reason to brag than anyone else. I was circumcised when I was eight days old, and I am from the nation of Israel and the tribe of Benjamin. I am a true Hebrew. As a Pharisee, I strictly obeyed the Law of Moses. And I was so eager that I even made trouble for the church. I did everything the Law demands in order to please God.**
>
> **Philippians 3:4–6 CEV**

This translation says that Paul "made trouble for the church," referring to his life as a Jew before he met Jesus on the Damascus Road. (See Acts 9:1–18.) That "trouble" included the murder of innocent men, women, and children—all in an effort to please the God of his Pharisaical religion. Now I have never seen anyone being killed physically by religious leaders, but I have witnessed the destruction of numerous people's lives by "religious" men who attempted to define what a person was required to do in order to be accepted by God. Sunday after Sunday, the souls of these poor individuals were burdened with standards impossible to attain by anyone other than Jesus Himself. After years of being subjected to this type of religious abuse, eventually many—including myself—collapsed under the weight of this burden because they could never attain the perfection that was demanded of them.

Now the apostle Paul was obviously capable of reaching a very high standard since "he did everything" the Law demanded. The question is, did Paul reach his goal? Was he able to "please God"?

He answers that question for us:

> **But Christ has shown me that what I once thought was valuable is *worthless* ... I could not make myself acceptable to God by obeying the Law of Moses.**
>
> **vv. 7,9 (emphasis added)**

Did you see that? All of that effort—worthless in the eyes of Jesus! As hard as Paul tried, he admitted that he could not make himself acceptable to God by keeping the Law. But he did not stop there. Let's continue reading verse 9:

> **God accepted me simply because of my faith in Christ.**

After all that striving, it was simply faith in Jesus that made Paul acceptable to God. Imagine the relief he must have experienced when he realized that he no longer needed to wear the robe of religion and tradition!

But what about *after* Paul became a Christian? Did he merely trade the Old Testament rules and regulations for a set of New Testament ones? This is an important question, because this is where we find ourselves today. As Christians, we are living under the New Covenant. Let's return to our passage in Philippians 3 and look to Paul's example to guide us.

The first thing I notice in this passage is that after Paul was born again, his goals changed. After Christ showed him that all of his previous efforts were worthless, Paul said:

> **Nothing is as wonderful as knowing Christ Jesus my Lord. I have given up everything else and count it all as garbage. All I want is Christ and to know that I belong to him.**
>
> **vv. 8–9**

As a Christian, Paul gave up his former life of trying to keep all the rules and even went so far as to call that lifestyle "garbage"! Now this did not mean that he quit trying to do right, but his goal became to know Christ, not keep the rules. He went on to say:

> **I have not yet reached my goal, and I am not perfect. But Christ has taken hold of me. So I keep on running and struggling to take hold of the prize.**
>
> **Philippians 3:12 CEV**

Notice that Paul admits that he was still not perfect. But that did not change the fact that he was accepted by God! Christ had taken hold of him, and he has taken hold of you too, dear sister, if you have received Him as Savior.

YOU ARE CHOSEN

You might be thinking, *Yeah, right. I can see that He has chosen you, and it is obvious that He chose the apostle Paul. But me ... I'm not so sure.*

These are not just my words. Jesus Himself is saying to you, "You did not choose Me, but *I chose you*" (John 15:16, emphasis added)! People have tried to turn this around by giving us the robe of religion and tradition. In wearing it, you may have thought that it was up to you to choose Jesus, but in reality, He chose *you! Yes, you!* Think of it. You have been chosen by the King of the universe! Even when you and I were covered by the filth of the world, He *chose us!* It may be true that you have chosen Jesus, but clearly He chose you first!

Jesus is not the only One who chose us. The apostle Paul explains that *God the Father* also chose us:

> **[In His love] He chose us [actually picked us out for Himself as His own] in Christ before the foundation of the world, that we should be holy (consecrated and set apart for Him) and blameless in His sight, even above reproach, before Him in love.**
>
> **Ephesians 1:4 AMP**

Before you even had the opportunity to "be good enough," even in your mother's womb, He chose you and loved you. And so you would have no doubt about it and so you could read it over and over and over, He recorded it in His Word: "Before I formed you in the womb I knew and approved of you" (Jer. 1:5 AMP).

What a glorious day it was when this truth finally broke through my darkness and I began to see the light. No longer did I have to strive to please Him. He had already approved of me and chosen me! And the same is true for you! He has chosen *you.*

MAKE IT PERSONAL

In the beginning, the devil destroyed God's relationship with man in the Garden of Eden, but through Jesus that fellowship has been restored. Our part is to simply believe this and receive it. One of my favorite things to do when I meet someone who has been hurt by legalistic religion is to say, "Just ask Jesus to reveal Himself to you. Then listen." And this is what I say to you. There are no rules or religious hoops you have to jump through. Just know that He loves you and chose you first; therefore, you are safe. It is nothing we take credit for. All we can do is simply say, "Yes, I accept what You did for me, Jesus. Thank You."

I encourage you, my dear sister, to take God at His Word and believe the love He has for you. If you have not already accepted His free gift of salvation, will you consider doing it now? As soon as you confess Jesus as your Lord and Savior, the Heavenly Father will snatch you from the kingdom of darkness and transfer you into the Kingdom of the Son of His love. (Col. 1:13.)

Today I look back on that old life of trying to keep a million rules and shake my head. With everything in me, I want to say to you to please quit trying to live up to what you think God wants you to do to please Him. He loves you and there are no rules except this one: Look into His eyes and just say, "Jesus, I love You and trust You. Please help me to do Your will." When I fell into the arms of Jesus with these same words, it was the most liberating thing I had ever done. When I realized *He* had already chosen me and that I was His special daughter—before my birth, before I even took one breath—I could finally relax and say, "I love You, Jesus," and mean it at a level I had never felt for any person on this earth.

WHAT IF I BLOW IT?

Let me encourage you that even the best of Christians blow it from time to time. As we saw earlier in this chapter, not even the apostle Paul could live a perfect life—and neither can you. Paul assured us that "all have sinned and fall short of the glory of God" (Romans 3:23). Every person who has lived on Planet Earth, except for Jesus Himself, has missed the mark.

What you must remember is that Satan is a legalist and he will quickly remind you of your faults and failings. In fact, the Bible describes him as the "accuser of our brethren" (Rev. 12:10). His number one objective is for you to doubt the Word of God and God's love for you. He wants you to run *from* God instead of *to* Him. But don't fall for it! When you mess up, turn in your Bible to 1 John 1:9:

If we confess our sins, He is faithful and just to forgive us our sins and to cleanse us from all unrighteousness.

I will tell you what I like to tell my children: When you confess your sins, it is like taking a bath with "Holy Ghost super soap." You become as clean as if you had never missed it in the first place.

Remember, you took off the robe of unforgiveness in the last chapter, so stop beating yourself up when you fail to be perfect, whether it is an attempt to please people or God. Your heavenly Father is already pleased with you. You are loved and approved just by trusting Jesus—period. No more striving is necessary. Will you accept it?

A NEW MOTIVATION

I am sure that you can tell that I am a fanatic when it comes to telling people that they do not have to obey a bunch of religious rules in order to please the Father. It is because I know the utter futility of it, after trying and failing for over twenty years to meet the standards placed upon me by people. And those people did not even know my Jesus! Nothing can compare to the peace I have experienced over these last eleven years, knowing that I am loved and accepted by Him, no matter what. It makes me smile just to think about it, and it is what I want for you.

When I finally did meet the real Jesus and got to know Him, I found that the motive behind my desire to please Him changed. Instead of feeling like I had to please Him in order to be accepted, I found that I desired to please Him because He loved me so much! It is similar to my relationship with my husband. I know that Dave loves me as much as any human possibly can; and because of that, I always *want* to please him. How much more do I desire to please Jesus who loves me with an everlasting love that cannot be measured in human terms!

My dear sister, I desire for you to come to know this same love and acceptance. In fact, I pray for you as the apostle Paul prayed:

> **May you be rooted deep in love and founded securely on love, that you may have the power and be strong to apprehend and grasp with all the saints [God's devoted people, *the experience of that love*] what is the breadth and length and height and depth [of it]; [that you may really come] to know [*practically, through experience for yourselves*] the love of Christ, which far surpasses mere knowledge [without experience].**
>
> **Ephesians 3:17–19 AMP (emphasis added)**

A GAME YOU WON'T MIND LOSING

Dave and I play a game where we ask each other, "How much do you love me?" Dave always declares himself the winner because when we were dating, he told me that he loved me before I told him. He loves reminding me of that fact. As one who never received that kind of unconditional love prior to meeting Dave, it makes me smile every time he says it to me.

Guess what? Jesus wants to play that game with you! But do you know who will always be the winner? You guessed it—Jesus will. According to 1 John 4:19, "We love Him because *He first loved us*" (emphasis added). Now that's a game none of us should mind losing!

Dear sister, get ready to take off the robe of religion and tradition this week. You can learn to receive His love for you, and in turn you will be free to love Jesus like never before. Love never fails. Since He truly loves you, you cannot fail when you depend on Jesus, His Word, and the Holy Spirit who lives inside you.

Week 3

Take Off the Robes of Religion and Tradition

Week 3, Day 1 — No Watered-Down Christianity

How many times have we asked our brothers or sisters in Christ or even a stranger where they go to church? Why would we even care where someone goes to corporate worship, except to quickly get an understanding of safe conversations to have about our belief systems? Wouldn't it be nice just to say, "Do you know Jesus?" We need to get deep in our spirits that knowing Jesus as our Savior is all that matters and then embrace each other with the love of the Lord.

Welcome to our third week of getting out of some clothes we have become very used to wearing. We are getting ready to get out of our so-called denominational robes of religion and tradition. Let's again put our focus on Jesus. Whenever we look at Jesus, we have to look at the Word of God.

Write out John 1:14:

_____

_____

_____

Write out 1 John 5:7:

_____

_____

_____

Write out Revelation 19:13:

_____

_____

_____

What do you find in common in all of these verses?

_____

_____

It is amazing how all of the verses speak of the Lord as the Word of God. Whenever we are in love with Jesus, we have to be in love with

His Word. There can be no separation of Jesus from the Word. We can hear the voice of the Lord clearly whenever we listen intently to the Word of the Lord.

Now, let's forget whether we are Pentecostal, Charismatic, Baptist, Methodist, Freewill Baptist, Missionary Baptist, Catholic, or whatever denomination we were raised up in. Let's look at Jesus to see what He says we need to do to get out of these old clothes. This week will be an intense one and one I feel will change many people's lives if they will get rid of their old mind-set about "church as usual."

Write your definition of the word "religion":

_____

_____

Write your definition of the word "tradition":

_____

_____

According to *Holman's Bible Dictionary,* the definition of "religion" is a relationship of devotion or fear of God or gods.[3] According to *New Webster's Dictionary and Thesaurus,* "tradition" means the belief, custom, narrative, etc. transmitted by word of mouth from age to age.[4]

Listen to this story about the way a young woman cooked her pot roast. I heard it many years ago when I first became an educator in the public schools. It was told at a workshop to make new educators question traditional educational techniques:

One young woman was cooking a pot roast the way she had seen her mom fix pot roast all of her life. The second step after washing the roast was to cut off about a half inch and throw it away. When the mother asked her daughter why she was cutting off the roast, she said it was because she was doing just as she had watched her do for years. Her mom's reply was that she cut off the roast because the pan she baked it in was small and she had to cut off a portion of the meat to make it fit. Then the mom told her daughter she had no need to cut off such beautiful meat.

Many times we do things just because it was placed in us and we watched our families worship for years with specific traditions and certain religious activities. It is time to ask if these traditions are biblical and actually working in our lives. Quit cutting off portions of the Word of God because this was how you were raised.

Read Matthew 15:1-9. Remember, this was after Jesus had done many miracles and been in His ministry for a while. Jesus had been coming against many traditions of the religious leaders of the day. The leaders did not have the authority of Jesus and surely were not laying hands on the sick and seeing them recover nor casting out demons.

---

[3]*Holman's Bible Dictionary,* 1173.
[4]*New Webster's Dictionary and Thesaurus,* 400.

Who were the religious leaders during the time of Christ?

_____

_____

What traditions did these leaders question Jesus about?

_____

_____

What was the reply of the Lord to these leaders?

_____

_____

We see Jesus using the Ten Commandments as His standard. However, the Jews of our Lord's time believed, in addition to the Ten Commandments, that there were oral laws given to Moses on Sinai and passed down by word of mouth until they reached the Council of Elders around 291 B.C. Many of these so-called laws had been written to allow them not to do as the Law of Moses specified. Jesus showed in this passage in Matthew that additions to the Word of God are a contradiction to the Word. Jesus refuted their argument about His disciples washing their hands with how the Jews of His time were adamantly disobeying the fifth commandment of honoring your father and mother. Jesus, the Word, loved the Word of God and would not in any way come against the Word of God.

Do you know the Word of God well enough to know whether you are following tradition or the actual Word? Be honest and ask the Holy Spirit to give you such a thirst for the Lord and His Word you will stop being deceived. Let's look in the eyes of Jesus and ask Him to help us to see what we need to keep in the Word that through tradition we have allowed to be cut off and thrown away.

Jesus came to give us life and to give it with great abundance. If you aren't living this abundant life, then maybe you have thrown away some of the Word of God that can give you the freedom you have been asking the Lord to give you.

Write out Matthew 4:4:

_____

_____

Write out a prayer to the Lord and ask the Holy Spirit to guide you into all truth so you can live out the abundant life and become so salty that others will want to taste the "living water" that Jesus said would come out of our spiritual bellies.

_____

_____

_____

God bless you. This week will liberate you tremendously. I love you and cannot wait to see you start unbuttoning these old clothes of tradition that have no power on anyone's life, especially yours. Get ready to walk in a new level of anointing and power promised in Mark 16:17-20. We will talk again tomorrow.

Week 3, Day 2 — Are You a Sheep or a Goat?

How would a Christian look in your eyes? Describe what a born-again believer would look like to you if you saw him or her in church on a Sunday morning.

Imagine that you are sitting next to a Christian. Describe how he or she is dressed and groomed in the space below:

_____

_____

_____

_____

Read Matthew 25:31-46.

How will the Son of Man separate the unbelievers from the believers?

_____

_____

In verse 45, whom did Jesus say if you blessed, you did it for Him?

_____

_____

How did you feel about reading over this passage of Scripture? Were you convicted over how you felt Jesus would judge our lives? Write your thoughts about this passage of Scripture:

_____

_____

_____

_____

Jesus obviously was a man of great action. We see through the Scriptures that He healed everywhere He went and people were greatly affected by His ministry. The word "Christian" means to be Christ-like.

What areas in your life need to be more Christian? Ask the Holy Spirit to show you areas you need to submit to the Word and write them below:

_____

_____

_____

Write out John 14:12:

_____

_____

_____

Jesus tells us we will do even greater things than He did while He was on the earth. Whenever I read this verse, I was amazed that as a Christian I have the ability to do even greater works than Jesus did. Jesus fed thousands, healed the sick, raised the dead, and did so many things the Apostle John said there would not be enough books to contain them if they were written out.

Where can you start showing the love of Jesus?

_____

_____

_____

Going back to Matthew 25 and seeing the separation of the sheep and the goats, we see that true believers are people of action. Please do not get me wrong and think I am saying we all have to have a food ministry or a prison ministry to be a sheep. However, there are ministries right in your area that would love for you to get involved, either through prayer, finances, or volunteering your time.

I believe Jesus was saying if you are a follower of Him, then you will realize you are to be affecting people's lives and bringing glory to God, the Father. We have to tell the world about Jesus and not only lead them to accept Jesus as their Savior, but have lives of action that display the love of Jesus.

Take time today and ask the Holy Spirit to show you areas you need to repent of and start living like a sheep, not a goat. One day we will all give an account of our deeds and every work will be tried by the fire of the Holy Spirit to see if our actions were to glorify God in our lives or another act of selfishness. We need to ask the Holy Spirit to open our eyes to the many hurting people around us.

Write out a prayer from your heart to the Lord about today's Bible study:

_____

_____

_____

_____

_____

Scripture says over and over again that a Christian is known by what he or she does. Let's throw off the robe of tradition of what a Christian should look like and get busy in the Kingdom of God being a "sheep" for Jesus.

I was raised on a farm and there are two major differences between a sheep and a goat. A sheep will obey and is very submissive. A goat is full of "buts" and will not obey but will give you a million reasons why he or she cannot obey. Let's get off the "buts" and be doers of the Word of God like James 1:22 tells us.

I have heard psychologists say again and again that people who battle depression cannot stay depressed if they will focus on helping others. Let's take off the robe of traditional Christianity and get free to help others.

We will talk more tomorrow and get a new outfit so we can live according to John 14:12. Once you are free from all of these robes, you will walk in such freedom everywhere you go. From the gas station to the grocery store you will see people's lives changed for Jesus!

I love you, my sisters, and have prayed over you already and know you are becoming free. We will talk again tomorrow, my sweet "sheep" in the Lord.

Week 3, Day 3 — The Word of God Heals — Part 1

When Jesus started His ministry as stated in Luke 4:16, He had just spent forty days in the wilderness, being tempted by the devil. Whenever we are ready to move to a new level, my sisters, there has to be a time of consecration and setting apart of one's life to hear from the Lord. If Jesus had to spend this much time fasting to overcome the enemy's lies, we know we should fast and pray on a regular basis.

Open your Bibles to **Luke 4:1-13**, read this section prayerfully, and meditate on what is going on with our Lord.

In verse 4, what did our Lord tell the devil we should live by?

_____

_____

In Jeremiah 1:9, what did the Lord place in Jeremiah's mouth?

_____

_____

How did Jesus answer the devil every time he tempted Him?

_____

_____

Whether you know it or not, every lie and accusation comes from the enemy. The Word speaks of Satan as the one who deceives the whole world. He takes this job very seriously and does not want you to be delivered and healed of your infirmities. However, the Word of God says it is the will of the Lord to heal His people. Jesus took your infirmities and you do not have to carry them anymore.

Write out Psalm 103:2-4:

_____

_____

_____

_____

_____

Write out Psalm 107:20:

_____

_____

Write out Jeremiah 17:14:

_____

_____

_____

Write out Matthew 18:20:

_____

_____

I have heard many people and leaders in the Church say that Jesus does not heal everyone. They quote many modern examples to back up their stories. However, we are adamant in our belief that the Word of God stands above every experience, story, or situation. There are over two hundred healing Scriptures in the Word of God. This is Good News to tell people they can be made whole in the name of Jesus.

Let me say something that you must get deep in your spirit. You may have to stand on the Word of God for quite sometime before your healing manifests. We have to have our minds totally renewed and get rid of all unbelief and tradition that say we cannot be healed.

Many times people have said to me that Isaiah 53:4-5 was only dealing with sin in the Old Testament and we do not have a right to stand on this scripture for our physical healing. Let's look at this verse in *The Amplified Bible*. *The Amplified Bible* goes back to the original languages the Bible was written in. The Bible tells us exactly what the words mean in the Hebrew and Greek. The Old Testament originally was written in the Hebrew and the New Testament in Greek. We cannot just translate a word into English and expect to understand the full meaning. *The Amplified Bible* explains specifically what these words mean:

"Surely He has borne our griefs (sicknesses, weaknesses, and distresses) and carried our sorrows and pains [of punishment], yet we [ignorantly] considered Him stricken, smitten, and afflicted by God [as if with leprosy].

"But He was wounded for our transgressions, He was bruised for our guilt and iniquities; the chastisement [needful to obtain] peace and well-being for us was upon Him, and with the stripes [that wounded] Him we are healed and made whole" (Isaiah 53:4-5).

In these verses, we see that Jesus took our sins or transgressions as well as our sicknesses, weaknesses, and distresses upon Himself on the cross. Therefore, my sisters, we do not have to carry those things anymore.

Write out Luke 4:18-19:

_____

_____

_____

_____

_____

Write out Matthew 8:16-17:

_____

_____

_____

Write out 1 Peter 2:24:

_____

_____

Hopefully, you are starting to be full of hope that you do not have to spend the rest of your life with mental or physical illness. Let me end today with a powerful testimony of a dear friend of mine.

Another friend, Rebekah my daughter, and I were visiting a woman who had been bedridden due to a car accident eight years ago. This pastor was hit by a drunk driver, and this caused severe damage to her spine. She has lived with constant pain and had migraines ever since this wreck. Also, she was operated on at Duke University for damage to the spinal cord. This woman of God has stood in agreement with her husband, family, and friends for eight years. She played healing scriptures over herself daily, took communion, and confessed the Word of God daily.

The night prior to this writing, she was completely healed and made whole. What a sight to see a woman who could not bend without intense pain dance before the Lord with tears streaming down her face. What a glorious sight to witness someone receive a healing they have sought diligently for years.

Remember, according to Romans 2:11, the Lord is not going to heal this woman of God, then not heal you. We serve a just God and He does not have favorites. We are all favorites in His eyes when we have Jesus in our hearts.

Start to believe for your family and yourself to be free and to be healed. We pray you will get out of the boat and get ready to meet Jesus on the water and do things such as you only dreamed of doing.

Write down something you feel you can start to believe Jesus to heal you of:

_____

_____

Now, find some scriptures to back up the healing you need. Search out the Word and confess these scriptures over yourself daily. We will be standing in agreement with you. Many people have been healed and made whole and you could be next. Play the Healing Scripture CD our ministry has produced. Hit the repeat button and it will play twenty-four hours a day.

Let's get out of some clothes we could call "unbelief" or "religion" after today's lesson. Stick with me, my dear sisters, and know you are going to become renewed in your mind as spoken of in Romans 12:2. Start unbuttoning those clothes of unbelief and doubt and let's get ready to receive the robe of faith to move forward for your miracle.

Lean not on your own understanding, but rest in the arms of Jesus and listen to His voice through His Word. Remember, He is your Daddy and He sent His Son to die so we could be set free. Be at peace and receive the words of life in Jesus' name.

Week 3, Day 4 — The Word of God Heals — Part 2

To some in the traditional church, it is a new mind-set to think that it is the will of God to heal His children. By healing I mean both physical and mental illness. Personally, I was healed of mental illness and have seen hundreds healed of physical illness right before my eyes. My dear sisters, this is good news. We can pray in faith and receive healing in the name of Jesus.

Take a few moments to bow your head and ask the Holy Spirit to show you an area in either your mind or your body that needs healing. Do you suffer from depression, anxiety disorders, panic attacks, low self-esteem, cancer, diabetes, or any other illness? Are there addictions in your life that you have battled for years? Be honest in your small groups, share your requests, have your sisters lay hands on you, pray, and believe for your miracle. Get in agreement with women of God and stand for your breakthrough with vehement faith that will never give up.

Fill in the blanks that follow as you are led by the Holy Spirit:

I am believing for healing for _____ in the name of Jesus.

Write out Matthew 18:18-20. (Use these verses when you pray together.)

_____

_____

_____

_____

_____

_____

Read the most famous prayer in the Bible — Matthew 6:9-13. Then, highlight verse 10, writing it below:

_____

_____

_____

Answer the following question honestly: Are there any sick people in heaven? We all know the answer to this question is an adamant NO! Therefore, we are in the will of God to ask for healing while on the earth. Step out in faith and ask the Lord to heal you. Believe as never before and wait for your miracle.

I believe you are almost ready to remove that old robe of tradition that says, "Sometimes God heals and sometimes He doesn't." I do not have the answer as to why some people stand for their healing and die anyway. I am not the judge and I would never accuse someone of not having enough faith. All I want to do is get you to see that the Word of God says He heals and give you hope to believe for your miracle. We have seen so many miracles in our ministry and you can look around all of the time and hear of miracles happening in the name of Jesus.

The Word of God says there is an appointed time to die. (Hebrews 9:27.) If it is not your appointed time, then stand in faith for the miracle you need. I stood on the Word awaiting the healing of my mind and emotions. I have said many times that I still have to stay in the Word to maintain this healing. I know what it feels like to not have a sound mind due to abuse. The fact that I am writing this Bible study as the Lord directs me is clear evidence of the healing power of God. Believe me when I say this is a miracle.

I agree with the Word of God that my Lord is not a respecter of persons. (Romans 2:11.) He is not going to heal me and say He likes Jennifer better, and therefore not heal another one of His children. That is not the God we serve. Favoritism is not fair play, and you do not have to fear the Lord loving one of His children over another one.

Tomorrow we will have our final day to get out of these old robes of religion and tradition and be freed of all doubt. I love you and look forward to our final day of getting out of this heavy, bulky robe.

Consider this chapter in our Bible study with much prayer and keep asking the Lord to verify what you are reading with His Word. Do not take someone else's word over the Word of God. Get into the Word of God, listen to the Healing Scripture CD, and hear for yourself all of the healing scriptures.

When the Lord started dealing with me on healing, I was amazed at all of the scriptures in the Word dealing with healing. However, my sweet sisters, we have an incredible Daddy in heaven who truly loves us, and we should not be shocked to learn that He desires to see us whole in body, soul, and spirit according to First Thessalonians 5:23 KJV: **"And the very God of peace sanctify you wholly; and I pray God your whole spirit and soul and body be preserved blameless unto the coming of our Lord Jesus Christ."**

Week 3, Day 5 — Jesus Still Heals!

Hang in there with me, my sisters, and let's join our faith together according to Matthew 18:20. Romans 10:17 says, **"So faith comes by hearing, and hearing by the word of God."**

Write out Hebrews 4:12:

_____

_____

_____

_____

_____

On our final day of realizing the need to get out of a religious mind-set, I want you to take the Word of God and cut off any tradition that says it is not the will of God to heal you and make you whole in any way. Let me say again, it is the will of God to see you healed, delivered, and walking in the abundant life Jesus died to give to each of His children. Let's allow the Word of God to heal and deliver us.

Write out Numbers 23:19:

_____

_____

_____

Write out Hebrews 13:8:

_____

_____

Write out Isaiah 53:5:

_____

_____

_____

_____

What do you think will block you from receiving healing from the Lord? (See Matthew 21:22.)

_____

_____

What do we need to move in to receive our miracles?

_____

_____

Write out your personal definition of "faith":

_____

_____

My dear sisters in Christ, I was raised in a religious cult and always just accepted what was presented from the pulpits I sat under as a little girl. From now on, let the Word of God give you answers.

There was a group of people who studied under the Apostle Paul called the Bereans who searched out the scriptures after Paul preached to make sure he was correct. I want you to do as the Bereans did, as we get out of our religious clothes. It is interesting how many answers you can receive when you ask people to give you their definition of "faith."

Again, let's see what the Word of God says about what faith is: **"Now faith is the assurance (the confirmation, the title deed) of the things [we] hope for, being the proof of things [we] do not see and the conviction of their reality [faith perceiving as real fact what is not revealed to the senses]"** (Hebrews 11:1 AMP).

Now, if you receive what the Word of God says when you move in faith, you will realize that Jesus paid it all on Calvary and you need to accept, by the grace of God, that you have a right to your miracle.

Within a month of this writing, I will have the title deed to my Yukon XL Denali. This means I will own it and BB&T has to give me the title of ownership. The car is mine and it has been paid in full.

How does this sound to you in dealing with the healing you desire? When I believed for the healing of my mind, I would speak verse after verse and say I was healed, even though I had no evidence or sign my mind was healed.

When we are believing and moving in faith, we do not look in the natural, we look to the final victory. I believed healing over depression, OCD, severe anxiety, and any of the other illnesses that had plagued me all of my life. I lived out this faith and the Word of God set me free.

Hang in there, believe, and stand on the Word no matter what the devil is telling you. You are healed and I am in agreement with you in the name of Jesus. Jesus healed you over two thousand years ago. Yes, the Lord does use doctors. Luke was a doctor. However, a physician is not the healer. Jesus is the Healer and He died for your healing.

I love you and I am glad you are removing your final robes of religion and tradition that have held you back for years from stepping out in faith. Now, stand tall and receive a nod from your Father in heaven to move in faith and believe for your miracle. I am rejoicing with you and I am so glad we have removed two more ugly robes as we get ready to see our Lord move mightily in our lives.

Next week, we will sit together and discuss getting out of two more robes we do not need to wear. Step out in faith with your sisters and let them lay hands on you for your healing. Jesus gave you the title deed to healing on Calvary. What a mighty God we serve!

Play the healing scriptures over yourself daily and confess them daily. You have to reach a point where you believe the Word of God over anything you see or feel. You can drive the enemy out of your life with the Word of God just like our Savior did, and be made whole in Jesus' name. Stand in agreement and watch the shackles of the mind and body fall from you.

Write out 2 Corinthians 10:4-5:

_____

_____

_____

_____

_____

_____

Now, let us stand up tall and remove these robes of religion and tradition. You can be free to be a part of the Body of Christ without any barriers, denominational guidelines, or boundaries.

Finally, let's get rid of the mind-set that Jesus will not heal His children. It is the will of God to heal you! Whenever I first began to believe it is the will of God to heal, I searched the Bible to find an example of Jesus not healing and I could not find one example. My sisters, stand on the Word as never before and believe for your personal healing.

I love you and I praise Jesus that you are free from the robes of religion and tradition. Enjoy your new freedom! We will remove two more robes next week — negativity and complaining.

Yes, Your Words Count!

Death and life are in the power of the tongue.
Proverbs 18:21 KJV

How many times have we heard the following saying: "Sticks and stones may break my bones but words will never hurt me"?

If ever there was a lie from the pit of hell, it is this. The reality is that negative words *do* hurt—badly. Although it might not be seen immediately, the effects are harmful and long lasting. In fact, if they are spoken often enough, especially by those who are in authority or whom we esteem, negative words have the power to absolutely destroy a human life.

I know ... from firsthand experience.

My earliest recollections of negative words being used against me began when I was four years old. Although I do not believe that she meant to hurt me, my grandmother told me a story many times and also took the opportunity to share it at every gathering with family and friends.

> Shortly after you were born, your dad came to the hospital to see you for the first time. As he peered into the bassinet, he said, "Well, that is the ugliest one we have had yet." Then when I arrived, he told me the same thing. And sure enough, your dad was right. You were the ugliest baby of all the children.

Time after I time when I heard this story I would chuckle as a way to cover up the pain. Inside, the words cut to the core of my being. Naturally, since I heard them so often, I believed them to be true.

I also remember many instances when I would be out and about with my dad. People would comment to him, "You sure have a cute little girl there." To that he would respond, "Well, you should see my daughter *Kathy*. Now *she* is the beautiful one in the family."

My looks were not the only area assaulted by the enemy. I was the youngest of the children in our family, and two of my older siblings were exceptionally bright. The leaders of our religious group bragged on them constantly, all the while I was struggling through elementary school. I remember being shy and scared. When I would try to sing with my family in church, I cried most of the time, terrified that I was not acceptable to God. Over and over the negative words spoken over me would replay in my mind: "You will never make it, Jenny. You are not pretty; you are not smart. You just don't fit into the system."

Fast forward to my college years. I will never forget the response of my family when I told them I wanted to try out for the Miss North Carolina Fourth of July beauty pageant. It was highly unusual for me to want to step out like this, but I was motivated. The grand prize was a scholarship that would enable me to return to college and fulfill my dream of graduating. But instead of receiving much needed encouragement from my family, I was met with this: "Jenny, your sister Kathy was asked to try out, but she doesn't think that she could win. You might as well forget it."

For once—just once—I wanted to prove them wrong. So despite tremendous anxiety, I decided to go for it. Imagine my family's shock as their shy little ugly duckling not only entered the pageant but won it! I was certainly thrilled with winning, but even that did not heal the wounds caused by years and years of negative words. I still saw myself as "the ugly child."

My family was not alone in their criticism. The leaders of our religious group never liked me and took every opportunity to put me down. It was common to hear them says thing like, "That Jennifer—you sure can't trust her. She isn't like anyone else in her family. She is sneaky and rebellious." More than once I heard that I was an embarrassment to my family because I could not seem to fit in. Other children even shunned me based upon the things I am certain that their parents said about me behind closed doors.

THAT WASN'T THE WORST OF IT

As awful as those examples were, the devil really brought out the heavy guns through the extended family member who sexually abused me for ten years, beginning when I was a very young. I specifically remember the summer I was around ten years old. Oh, how I wanted to be the best that I could be for Jesus, and I knew that He did not like the dreadful things that Joe made me do. As was often the case in the summer, my siblings and I were left on the family farm to do chores while our parents worked in town. One afternoon I heard the familiar sound of a loud muffler as a car made its way down the long dirt road to our house. I knew it was Joe and that he had come to take me back to the mobile home where he lived with my sister Sue. Since he was part of the family, no one thought anything about it, or at least no one took the time to find out why he wanted to spend so much time with me.

That day after he finished his disgusting deeds, I said to him, "Joe, I want to become a Christian and have Jesus in my life, but I feel dirty. Can you please stop all of this, so Jesus will accept me?"

His reply sends shivers up my spine even now, all these years later. He said, "What are you talking about? You *make* me do it. You are the reason that I do all of these things to you. I'm tellin' you right now. You'd better not tell Sue, or she will hang you upside down on the clothesline and let the blood drain out of you like those chickens you saw hanging after we cut their heads off. If people knew what you make me do, you would get in more trouble than you can imagine."

Those chilling words stopped me in my tracks. I believed him, and over the next four years as he continued to violate me, I never again tried to stand up to Joe. And I was convinced that Jesus would *never* want me after all the things I "made" my brother-in-law do. After all the damaging things that had been said to me, I truly believed that I was ugly and bad.

Looking back, I can see that devil knew I was marked by God to be the first in my family to be delivered from the religious cult we were in. To this day, I am still praying for the others. The devil also knew that God had destined for me to become an evangelist who would expose his evil deeds of darkness. I understand now why he set out while I very young to systematically chip away at my soundness of mind. But praise the living God, my Jesus set me free and restored not only my mind, but my entire being. He knew that my heart was crying out for Him, and He never gave up on me.

PROPHECY FULFILLED

Unfortunately, even after I was free of Joe's abuse, many dark years still lay ahead. All of those negative words had taken root in me, and I became a grown woman with absolutely no boundaries or self-respect. I know now that I was actually wearing "the robe of negative words and complaining" that had been placed on me by family and the members of our religious system. Practically every word that came out of my mouth was permeated with negativity. Because this robe distorted the truth, I always saw the glass half empty, never half full. Consequently, I never talked about how things could get better but always complained about how bad they were. Without realizing it, I was allowing my words to imprison me in a miserable and defeated life. A spiritual law was at work, according to Jesus:

"For by your words you will be justified, and by your words you will be condemned."

Matthew 12:37

My own words were condemning me to a life that I hated, and I didn't even know it.

People who have never suffered abuse are always perplexed when they hear of a battered woman dropping the charges and returning to the abuser. To a healthy, whole person, it makes no sense at all; however, as one who has lived through that hell myself, I know just how easy it is. Before I met my husband, Dave, I was in two very abusive relationships. The two men beat me and called me filthy, perverted names; yet, over and over I returned to them like a whipped and abused puppy. When one of my family members asked why I would ever allow a man to beat me, my reply was, "After being sexually abused, this is a piece of cake."

A piece of cake? How is *that* for distorted reality? Do you see how the devil twists the truth! Yet that is how I saw it. Compared to what I had suffered before, this was a big improvement. And after all the things I had done, who was I to think that I deserved better?

I believe that this was a culmination of all the threats and degrading things that were spoken over me as a child. What a perverted man and other people said about me shaped the way I thought of myself, putting another spiritual law into motion. Proverbs 23:7 says, "For as he thinks in his heart, so is he." I never looked in the mirror and saw an attractive woman worthy of respect. Instead I saw a filthy piece of trash who was hiding the deep dark "truth." Because of these lies, I was willing to do anything to be accepted, even if it cost me my self-respect and meant enduring personal injury.

Unfortunately, my experience is not unique. Millions of women around the globe have experienced—and are currently experiencing—these same horrors and worse. As in my case, I believe negative words spoken by parents or other significant people have played a large role in shaping the destinies of these women. Once a person's self-worth is destroyed, the stage is set for the devil to usher his abusers right in.

SOMEONE YOU CAN COUNT ON

Many times words have so scarred us that even talking about them can be painful. This was the case with a beautiful twenty-one-year-old woman whom I met recently. In tears, she lamented the fact that it had been terribly difficult for her to trust her heavenly Father. As she began to tell me her story, it was easy to see why. The enemy had skillfully set up circumstances while she was a child to twist the way she viewed God.

It began when the girl was young and her mother passed away at an early age. At the close of the funeral, her father told her that he had to leave for a while but he would come back to get her.

But he never returned.

This was only the beginning of many broken promises by the man whose job it was to comfort her and watch over her. Many, many times the pattern would play out: The girl's father would promise to come see her. She would excitedly wait for hours, hoping that *this time* he would keep his word. But each time, he broke his promise. Continual disappointment chipped away at her ability to trust anyone, especially the One known as the heavenly Father. Why would He be any different? I knew that only the power of God and a revelation from the Holy Spirit could heal this woman and enable her to trust Him.

Praise God, He is in the miracle-working business, and no case is too difficult for Him. In a single moment, He can undo years of damage by causing us to see things in a new way. He exposes Satan's lies and enables us to see the strategies that he has used against us. And this is what He did for this lovely young woman. As the heavenly Father healed her broken heart and she experienced His pure love, she *knew* everything was going to be all right. For the first time in her life, she had Someone she could trust.

About a month after I prayed with this woman, I ran into her and was delighted to see that she was still beaming with the joy of the Lord. She shared that every day she was coming to a deeper revelation that God is utterly trustworthy and that He always keeps His Word.

Have you been lied to? Have people let you down? If so, the following is some of the best news you will ever hear:

> **God is no mere human! He doesn't tell lies**
> **or change his mind. God always keeps his promises.**
>
> **Numbers 23:19 CEV**

What an awesome God He is!

JACOB AND ESAU

The fact that words are powerful is not a new doctrine. Think back to Genesis 1, when God created the world. How did He do it? Through the power of the spoken word. You see, He established this principle at the very dawn of time itself. Let's look at the story of Jacob and Esau found in Genesis 27, where this truth is illustrated in a profound way.

Jacob and Esau were the twin sons of Isaac and Rebekah, Jacob being his mother's favorite. When Isaac was nearing death, Rebekah overheard him say to Esau,

> **"Go out to the field and hunt game for me. And make**
> **me savory food, such as I love, and bring it to me that I**
> **may eat, that my soul may bless you before I die."**
>
> **Genesis 27:3–4**

Note those words, "that my soul may bless you." Immediately upon hearing this, Rebekah ran to inform her beloved Jacob. You see, the "blessing" was a powerful pronouncement that resulted in success in every part of the recipient's life. Typically it was reserved for the first-born son, which was Esau.

Jacob recognized the power of that blessing—the power of those words—so he and his mother conspired against Esau to swindle him out of it. The aged Isaac suffered from poor eyesight, and Jacob used this weakness to his advantage. In order to mimic the hairy arms of his brother, Jacob dressed himself in animal skins. He prepared his father's favorite meal, then tricked his father into speaking the blessing over him.

When the deed came to light, Esau begged his father to bless him also. But it was too late. That blessing had been pronounced upon Jacob, and nothing could undo it. Job very accurately explained this principle:

> **You shall also decide and decree a thing, and it shall**
> **be established for you; and the light [of God's favor] shall**
> **shine upon your ways.**
>
> **Job 22:28 AMP**

Dear sister, there is tremendous power in what we speak and what is spoken over us. The spoken word *establishes* the very thing said— first in the spirit realm, then eventually in the natural. In the case of Jacob and Esau, Jesus had not come yet; therefore, no one had the authority to undo the thing that was decreed.

But such is not the case for us, dear sister. Jesus has come and He triumphed over the devil, winning back the authority that Adam lost in the Garden of Eden. Then Jesus transferred that authority to us, His blessed children. We are no longer bound to the death sentence placed upon us by the negative words of ourselves and others. By the blood of Jesus, we can break the power of every lie of the enemy and pronounce the blessing of God in its place!

MORE SCRIPTURAL FOUNDATION

When I began studying the Bible about the power of words, I discovered the following passage:

I call heaven and earth as witnesses today against you, that I have set before you life and death, blessing and cursing; therefore choose life, that both you and your descendants may live.

Deuteronomy 30:19

By this we know that living a life of blessing is a choice. Join me and "choose life" by speaking life-giving words from the Bible. Refuse to allow words of death to cross your lips.

As I studied further about "blessing and cursing," I was amazed to read what *Holman's Bible Dictionary* says about the power of words:

According to the Old Testament thought patterns the formally spoken word had both an independent existence and the power of its own fulfillment. The word once spoken assumed a history of its own, almost a personality of itself. The word also had the power of its own fulfillment. Both of these concepts are fundamental to understanding Isaiah's emphasis on God's Word in Isaiah 55:10–11. The Word of God exists as a reality and has within itself the power of its own fulfillment.[5]

In *The Living Bible*, the passage referred to in Isaiah states:

As the rain and snow come down from heaven and stay upon the ground to water the earth, and cause the grain to grow and to produce seed for the farmer and bread for the hungry, so also is my Word. I send it out and it always produces fruit. It shall accomplish all I want it to and prosper everywhere I send it.

Do you see how important it is to speak God's Word? He literally watches over it to make sure that it comes to pass in our lives! One way He does this is through His angels, as stated by the Psalmist.

Bless the Lord, you His angels,
Mighty in strength, who perform His word,
Obeying the voice of His word!

Psalm 103:20 NASB

These are just a few of the many verses that reveal the importance of speaking God's Word and what we can expect as a result.

---

[5]*Holman's Bible Dictionary*, 199.

PRACTICAL APPLICATION

When I first began learning these things, I naturally became more aware of what I was saying. At the time I had a very active two-year-old boy who loved to climb on the furniture. Concerned that he might hurt himself, it was common for me to say things like, "Get down from there or you are going to break your neck!"

When Rebekah came along, her brother was still a toddler—not an easy time of life for a mother. Many a day I would call Dave to complain, "These kids are driving me crazy." It is no small coincidence that it was during this time in my life when I mentally broke down. My words were not solely responsible for that crisis, but it is plain to see that they played a part.

Little did I realize that the robe of negative words and complaining were shaping the very world I lived in. It was rare to hear something positive from me. I remember when Dave built us our beautiful home. Where I should have been overjoyed, I saw every single flaw and was quick to tell Dave about it. Why were all of these negative words flying out of my mouth? Let's let Jesus answer this question.

"But those things which proceed out of the mouth come from the heart, and they defile a man."

Matthew 15:18

The robe of negative words and complaining had distorted the view I had of myself and everything around me. Consequently, my words were filled with negativity, which in turn continually defiled me. I was trapped in an ever-darkening downward spiral.

A NEW WAY OF LIFE

Thankfully a new day dawned when I met Jesus and He healed me. As I began drinking the living water of the Word of God, it started flushing all of that negativity out of me. No longer saddled by that old robe, I began to see things from God's perspective. When I started studying the Bible, I was amazed at the number of verses that had to do with the power of words. I realized in a hurry that it was time for me to start using this principle to my advantage, and I began speaking words of life over all the things that my words had previously cursed.

I remember the day I asked Dave to forgive me for all the hateful and mean things I had said over him and our marriage. I repented and told him that the Holy Spirit had convicted me through the Word of God and now I was going to speak the Word of God over our marriage, our children, and our companies. And wow, did things ever change! Immediately we began to see a difference around our house.

When little David crawled upon the couch, I now said, "Honey, get down from there and be careful." When he hit his baby sister, instead of telling, "You are being a bad boy," I began saying, "David, you are a good boy and good boys do not hit their little sisters." When I realized what I had done to my family due to all of the darkness that was in me, I asked my children to forgive me. Many a night I prayed over them when they were asleep, and through the power of the blood of Jesus, I cancelled the power of my negative words. Next I prayed for God to heal their wounded spirits, then I took the Word of God and decreed and declared blessings over their lives.

Today I daily maintain the spiritual atmosphere of our home by making sure we continually speak blessings. In addition, we have learned *not to receive* words spoken by others when they are negative. What a joy it is to hear my husband taking advantage of this principle. Every morning, if he is not away on business, he stands outside the doors of our children's bedrooms as they are getting ready for school and speaks blessings over their lives. We have also taught our children to speak blessings over themselves and to decree and declare what they know the Lord has called them to do in life. They are confident in Him that they are going to reach their destinies, and if you are around them long enough, you will hear it from their own lips.

WHAT ABOUT YOU?

Dear sister, I want to encourage you to begin listening to the words that you speak. Do they line up with the truth of God's Word? If not, ask the Holy Spirit to help you put a guard over your mouth and begin filling your mind with the goodness of the Bible. Jesus said, "The words that I speak to you are spirit, and they are life" (John 6:63). When we fill our mouths with God's Word, we quit reaping death as we used to and begin experiencing life in all its fullness.

What words do you speak over your children? Ask the Holy Spirit to help you recognize any harmful words before you say them. Choose instead to speak words that encourage and lift up. When you blow it, which we all do, be quick to apologize to your dear children, plead the blood over those words to cancel their power, then pronounce a blessing over them.

What words do you speak over your husband? Do you complain to your friends about his faults and failings? Do you remind him of them? Dear sister, the Lord has ordained that your husband become a mighty man of God! Yes, *your* husband. I urge you to learn what God says about him and begin speaking those words by faith. It will put an end to the negative cycle, and you will be astounded as you witness God bringing to pass His Word in your husband's life.

Single sister, I urge you to do the same. Look up the directives that God has given husbands in His Word, such as in Ephesians 5:

> **Husbands, love your wives, just as Christ also loved the church and gave Himself for her ... Husbands ought to love their own wives as their own bodies; he who loves his wife loves himself. For no one ever hated his own flesh, but nourishes and cherishes it, just as the Lord does the church.**
>
> **vv. 25,28–29**

Begin decreeing this type of husband for yourself, and do not settle for less. You are God's handmaiden, and He wants only the best for you. Marriage is one of His most wonderful blessings, and by speaking words of life, you can create your own Garden of Eden, right in your own home.

This week, dear sister, we are going to learn how to take off the robe of negative words and complaining. Get ready to begin a whole new way of life as you learn what the Word of God has to say about you. As you begin to fill your mouth with the good and true things that He says, you will find blessings overtaking you in every area of your life.

Week 4

Take Off the Robes of Negative Words and Complaining

Week 4, Day 1 — Your Words Impact You and Others!

This week I truly want you to submit yourself to the Holy Spirit and allow Him to convict you of the robes of speaking negative words and complaining. From this day forward, I want you to be aware of the words you speak over yourself and even over family and friends. It is amazing how, when one listens and speaks the Word of God, we stop all the negative and complaining words.

For years I have heard the power of our words over our life in the secular world and easily believed the concept of "self-fulfilling prophecy." This concept says that what you say over a child will cause him to live out what was spoken over him. For example, if you tell even an intelligent child that he or she is dumb, he or she will believe this and never excel in academics or probably not any other area until those words are stopped in a miraculous way.

To a child, what a parent speaks over him or her is the truth. As I write this study, with my ten-and twelve-year-old children asleep, I realize the impact of my words even more.

In today's society, we tend to believe secular therapists and try to do as they say before we accept the Word of God as truth in our every-day lives. In fact, why are there drugstores on every corner? Because America is the number one nation in the use of antidepressants by adults and Ritalin by children. At the time of this writing, there are four million children in America who are on Ritalin. I use these examples because the Word of God has much to say about being healed and it is time we believe the Word. I am not against medicine or physicians. Luke was a physician, and our God gives men wisdom to develop drugs to help His people.

Over the next week, I want you to listen to how you speak. Pray, "Holy Spirit, let me become aware of my speech. Does it edify me and my family or tear us down?" Let's start speaking the Word of God over ourselves, over our marriages, and over our children. I can assure you, the local drugstore will have fewer customers immediately!

Read Genesis 1:1-31 prayerfully.

In verse 2, what was hovering over the face of the earth?

_____

_____

In verse 3, what did God do to cause light?

_____

_____

Write down the numbers of the verses in this chapter that contain the phrase, "Then God said."

_____

_____

Write out Genesis 1:26:

_____

_____

_____

_____

We are made in the image of God. God told Adam to name all of the cattle, the birds of the air, and the beasts of the field. Immediately, God had Adam use the power of his words to name things.

Your words are very powerful, my sisters, and I want you to realize this is how we are designed. Personally, I realize how powerful words are and will not allow my husband or children to confess any negative words over our family, friends, ministry, or companies.

As I was writing this week about words, I heard a true story about how words spoken can have a powerful impact on lives. While running errands one day, I ran into an old friend. I asked her how a child she knew had dealt with the issue of her dad's suicide. She said people had always said about him that women would cause his death. When they found the suicide note, it was discovered that he had taken his life over a woman. I am not saying people caused this man's death, but he had heard this all of his adult life and it happened. Remember, words are powerful!

Let's look at an example of the famous singer, Elvis Presley. It has been told and recorded that all of his life he confessed that he would die at the same age of his mother. He did die at the same age his mother was when she died. The world says "coincidence," but I say, "Your words are powerful!"

Let's look at some verses to back up what I am teaching.

Write out Proverbs 18:21:

_____

_____

_____

_____

Write out Numbers 14:28:

_____

_____

_____

_____

Write out Proverbs 18:20:

_____

_____

_____

Write out Proverbs 6:2:

_____

_____

_____

_____

Now, my dear sisters, we will stop here for today. You have an assignment to become more aware of your words. If you have children, listen to the words they are saying over themselves. If you are married, listen to the words coming out of your husband's mouth. At this point, do not correct anyone but yourself. Just be a good listener and allow the Holy Spirit to tune you in to the negative words coming out of your family's mouth and your own mouth.

We will end this lesson with four verses that I have used often in my life. When you get up each morning, speak these verses over yourself. If you wish to be creative, type them out and put them on your mirror or night stand, and let these personalized scriptures be the first words out of your mouth.

For I know the thoughts the Lord thinks toward me — thoughts of peace and not of evil — to give me a future and a hope — Jeremiah 29:11.

My steps are ordered by the Lord, and He delights in my way — Psalm 37:23.

Jesus only is my rock and my salvation. He is my defense for each day. I shall not be greatly moved — Psalm 62:1-2.

I am so loved by Jesus and I love Him because He first loved me — 1 John 4:19.

My sisters, I love you and know you are on the path of removing the robes of negative and complaining words. Remember to read your scriptures and listen to your words and the words of your family.

Week 4, Day 2 — Words Are Powerful!

When the Holy Spirit convicted me of how powerful our words are through His Word and His servants over ten years ago, it was like a light bulb went off in my head. I have already prayed over you, my dear sisters in Christ, that you will come to this realization as we get ready to remove your robes of negative and complaining words.

Many times I have quoted Proverbs 18:21 to my family and ministry partners that life and death are in the power of the tongue. This is both a New and Old Testament concept.

Write out Matthew 15:11:

_____

_____

Write out Mark 7:20:

_____

_____

Write out Mark 11:23:

_____

_____

_____

_____

Write out Matthew 12:37:

_____

_____

Jesus was very careful to speak only the things He heard His Father in heaven speak. Jesus is our great example. We need to speak as He did. Jesus was the Word of God in the flesh. We are to speak things that line up with the Word of God.

Now, let me say right now as you begin to take off the robes of negative and complaining words that we have all made mistakes and will continue to do so until we get to heaven. When I say things I shouldn't say, I hear myself saying, "Forgive me, Lord! I make those words null and void in the name of Jesus." Then I know those words have lost their power. Through Calvary, Jesus has given us the authority that was stolen from us in the Garden of Eden and we can cancel our words out when we know we have made mistakes.

Let's look at more scriptures related to the words of our mouth.

Write out Ephesians 5:19:

_____

_____

Write out Ephesians 4:29-31:

_____

_____

_____

_____

_____

Write out Psalm 19:14:

_____

_____

Let's end today's lesson with this thought. Why do you think Romans 10:10 says, "By your confession you have been saved"? Let's go back to Genesis and again read how we are made in the image of God. Now, if you cannot be saved without confession, why do you think you can live an abundant life without confession?

Words are very powerful and I want you to say only positive things over your life, family, finances, and everything that concerns you. Stop destroying your blessing with your own words! Remember, life and death are in the power of your tongue.

Let's take off these ugly robes and start speaking blessings over everyone around us. Yes, it will seem very weird at first, but it works and it is biblical and correct.

Believe me, you will gladly throw off these robes and rejoice! I love you very much. Hang tight! I promise at the end of this seven-week journey you will rejoice that you hung in there with me and the Holy Spirit, who I know has guided this Bible study.

Week 4, Day 3 — What Is Your Confession?

My dear sisters, I pray you are getting a different view of your words and how powerful they are. In fact, your words may be hindering the miracle you need and the abundant life promised to you in John 10:10.

Let's start today's lesson with a lesson I learned from a Jewish girl I met at Wrightsville Beach, North Carolina. Whenever I saw this beautiful young lady outside of a popular store, I felt led by the Holy Spirit to spend some time with her. I asked her if she knew Jesus as her Lord and I began to ask her about her faith. She told me she did not believe in Jesus as the Son of God. She told me she was Jewish and they were still waiting for the Messiah. However, she was very receptive to me. I did not get to lead her to the Lord. Yet, I planted some serious seeds and look forward to seeing her in heaven.

Many times I think about the Apostle Paul and how he said he planted, Apollos watered, and God gave the increase. This young Jewish girl did give me insight into words and how powerful words are in our lives. I asked her if Jews believed the words they speak over their lives and family would come to pass. She was very adamant and told me she had always been raised not to speak negative words over her life or her family's life. She said they understood that our words are very powerful and her father spoke a blessing over her life every Friday. I was so amazed and just kept thinking how I needed to be so careful in speaking over my children, my marriage, and everything concerning my life.

I have asked other Jewish people this question and they are always amazed that Gentiles in America do not realize how serious our words are.

Write a prayer of repentance for using negative and complaining words, and ask the Lord to open your eyes to the truth of your words speaking either life or death.

_____

_____

_____

_____

What are some words that were spoken over your life that really hurt you?

_____

_____

_____

_____

What are some words that were spoken over your life that were very kind?

_____

_____

_____

_____

Let's look over more verses dealing with this subject.

Read Hebrews 3:1-2 and fill in the blank that follows: Jesus is the High Priest of our _____.

What is the Lord intervening on your behalf as you confess negative words over your life? Pay attention to how you discipline your children with your words. Since I have become very aware of my words, I have changed how I correct my children with my words. Instead of saying, "Rebekah, why are you so disobedient and dishonoring to me?" I find myself saying, "Rebekah, you are such an obedient child. Why did you choose to make the wrong choice this time?" We can discipline our children with words that bring great honor and make them want to do better.

Think about the way you talk to your spouse. This one was a big one for me, and I know Dave was so glad when the Lord convicted me over my words dealing with him. Instead of yelling, "How could you be so insensitive and not care for my feelings?" I hear myself saying, "Dave, you are such a great husband. Did you realize this action made you seem insensitive? Let's get this straight!"

Now, my sisters, I wish I could tell you I do this all the time, but I do not. The Holy Spirit is helping me daily and I feel even as I am writing this Bible study that I am still removing this robe. Hallelujah to the Lamb of God! There was a time when I could just say anything and truly did not believe my words made a difference.

Say this with me: *I believe the Word of God and know that the power of life and death lies in the tongue. In the name of Jesus, I remove these robes of negative and complaining words. Through the power of the Holy Spirit, I will say kind things over myself, my family, and my friends. I believe I have received the removal of these robes. Amen!*

Let Jesus be the High Priest of your good confession. We will talk again tomorrow about the robe of complaining. I know you have come a long way in this area and I high five you on your progress!

Week 4, Day 4 — By All Means, Stop Complaining!

Did you know the word "complain" in the Hebrew means to actually remain? Wow! That will be an eye opener as we begin to look at the robe of complaining. "You mean every time we complain on something, Jennifer, we are actually staying right where we are?" Yes!

Remember the children of Israel traveling in the wilderness for forty years when it was only a few days' journey to the promised land? What kept them out in the wilderness when they could be in the land promised to them from the time of their father Abraham? It was their harsh words about the Lord and not believing His promise to them. If you want to know what you truly believe, look at the following verse:

Write out Matthew 15:18:

_____

_____

_____

This reminds us of our negative words, but it also reminds us that we are speaking those things that are actually within us. This is why when someone excuses himself for cussing in front of me and says those words slipped, I know they just lied to me. Things do not just slip out of our mouths. We have to have it within us to come out of us.

Now, let's look at the children of Israel and how complaining kept them out of the promised land.

Read Numbers 14:1-35.

In verses 1-4, what are the children of Israel doing against Moses and Aaron and God?

_____

_____

In verse 27, what does the Lord say the children of Israel have done against Him?

_____

_____

What does the Lord say about Caleb and Joshua?

_____

_____

Remember, my sisters, the Lord had done many miracles in Egypt and in the wilderness and these people were acting as if the Lord had taken them out of a five-star resort instead of out of slavery. Think about us. We were taken out of the kingdom of darkness and put into the marvelous Kingdom of God, and we dare not raise our voices or complain against our God!

Write out 1 Peter 2:9:

_____

_____

You have been so blessed at salvation you should have the same spirit in you to say, "Give me that mountain!" as Caleb told Joshua when Israel finally went into the promised land when he was in his eighties.

What are the mountains in your life that you need to realize the Lord has already conquered through Calvary?

_____

_____

_____

_____

Watch your words against the Lord and stop your complaining or you will keep remaining. Stop complaining about your husband, your job, your children, and yes, even your church. You need to go into prayer and ask the Lord, first and foremost, to forgive you, and then make a conscious effort to say good things or keep your mouth very quiet about the situations that concern you. Jesus said He would never leave you or forsake you. Believe this and start talking like a believer, not a complainer.

My sweet sisers in Christ, you can do all things through Jesus who strengthens you! We have all been complainers and we have all made some serious mistakes with our words. Remember, there is now no more condemnation to those of us in Christ Jesus according to Romans 8:1. Do not receive condemnation over today's study. Instead, receive liberty and praise the Lord.

You are living for a God who gives you mercy every day. I love the verses in Psalm 136 because they say we serve the God of a million chances.

Let's take those mountains today and use our words to cause us to get into our promised land of marriage, child rearing, financial freedom, and other things you are believing for instead of complaining against. Start unbuttoning the robes of negative words and complaining. We will remove them tomorrow in Jesus' name.

I love you. You are getting free to be the woman God created you to become!

Week 4, Day 5 — Speak the Truth and the Truth Only!

This is our final day to completely destroy the stronghold of negative and complaining words. I am excited to know God is able to do abundantly above all we can think or ask. (Ephesians 3:20.)

As I write this lesson, I can hear you in your small groups saying that you had no idea words were so powerful and how you have been misusing them. This is a road the Lord had to deliver me from, and I am so excited your deliverance is today. Whatever you have done in the past, remember we serve a God of restoration. We serve a God who can take all the years the devil had you deceived and make each new day better than you could even imagine. Now, let's get to work on getting out of this robe.

Write out Joel 2:25-27:

_____

_____

_____

_____

_____

You serve a God who can restore all those years the locusts have eaten out of your life. I do not care if you are fifteen or ninety-five! Remember, Caleb got his promise when he was eighty years old! Let's take back what the devil has stolen out of your life and confess "thus says the Lord" over you and your family and watch things change.

As I had to admit with the fifteen pounds I had gained over three years, this did not happen overnight and they will not come off overnight. Consistently speak the Word of God over your situation and say positive words over and over to start seeing a change. Let's look once more at the Word of God and see that the Lord does not take it lightly when we complain about Him.

Read Malachi 3:13-18.

What is the first thing you notice when you read this portion of Scripture?

_____

_____

Have you said in the past, "It is useless to serve God"?

_____

_____

In verse 16, what was written before the Lord?

_____

_____

There are times when the enemy will try to convince us that serving the Lord does not pay off and we will not reap our reward! Do not listen to that liar. Only believe the Word of God. You have to do and say what the Lord says over your life and stand on the Word of God no matter what. I am a living testimony of the power of the Word and words spoken from our mouths.

The Lord has blessed me and my family in ways I could not even imagine. Eleven years ago, my marriage was falling apart, I was suicidal, and everything I touched was crumbling in front of my face. Then

I received Jesus and chose to believe the Word of God over everything that was in front of me. Next, I spoke the Word of God over the issues that needed to be changed. Now, I am getting ready to celebrate my fifteenth wedding anniversary and living the abundant life promised in John 10:10.

God has blessed me with the great honor of being an evangelist of the gospel of Jesus Christ. Eleven years ago, believe me, I would have been your last choice to spread the Good News about Jesus!

My sisters, take off the ugly cloaks of negative and complaining words and get ready to receive the robe of the Word of God! Make a conscious effort to say what the Word of God says and not what you feel or see.

As you finish this last paragraph on these ugly robes of negative and complaining words, sit up straight in your chair and get ready to discard these robes, never to put them back on again. Repeat the following prayer with me now:

Father, in Jesus' name, forgive me for all the negative and complaining words I have said against You, my family, or anyone else. I repent of sinning by using my own mouth. Thank You, Lord Jesus. I receive Your forgiveness for my mistakes with the words of my mouth. Anoint me to speak Your words and only edifying words over myself, my family, and friends.

I believe in the power of the blood of Jesus to erase those habits of negative and complaining words coming out of my mouth. Holy Spirit, make me aware of the power of my words and Your words in my life. I break these robes of negative and complaining words from my life and take Your Word in Hebrews 4:12 to cut off these robes in the supernatural to no longer hinder me in my walk with You, Lord Jesus. Thank You, Lord, for setting me free. I can hardly wait to receive the beautiful robe of righteousness in three weeks (although I know I became the righteousness of You, Father, through Jesus Christ the moment I was born again — 2 Corinthians 5:21).

Anoint me to finish this study and pray for my sisters who are in this study with me. I love You, Daddy. Thank You for sending Your Son to die for me so I can enter the promised land You have provided for me and my family. In the name of Jesus, my Savior, and the High Priest of my confession. Amen.

How do you feel, my sisters? You have just prayed deliverance over your life. I know the angels are preparing a beautiful robe of powerful and edifying words to place on you. I love you and look forward to taking off two more pieces of clothing next week — clothing not suitable for daughters of the King!

Week 5

Mercy Said No

Oh, give thanks to the Lord, for He is good!
For His mercy endures forever.
Psalm 136:1

Mercy said no. You might wonder, *What do you mean by that?* It means a great deal to me personally, which I will explain, but "Mercy Said No" is actually the title of a song sung by Larnelle Harris that makes me weep every time I hear it. The following lines in particular minister tremendous comfort and encouragement to my heart:

Mercy said no

I'm not going to let you go

I'm not going to let you slip away

You don't have to be afraid.

I guess the reason the words are so significant to me is that I am profoundly aware—and eternally grateful—that no matter what, Mercy Himself, the Lord Jesus, will never let me go. But I have not always known this. For years I wore the robe of judgment and criticism, and it prevented me from believing that Jesus could even accept me, much less that He would want to hold on to me or calm my fears. Because of my past, I was fully persuaded that I was doomed to receive His judgment.

How About You?

No doubt you've heard—or have even said yourself—the phrase, "Lord, have mercy." But what does that mean to you? Is it a sincere prayer or just a casual response to frustrating circumstances? I think that these words have been said so commonly that they have lost their true meaning in most people's minds. I want to propose to you that they make up one of the most powerful prayers a person can pray.

Before I explain, I want to ask you some questions. Who is Jesus *to you?* Do you know Him as your merciful Savior? When you think of the heavenly Father, do you envision the God whose mercy endures forever? Or are you like I was, terrified that the wrath of God is waiting for an opportune moment to zap you for your many sins, shortcomings, and failures?

Let me assure you, dear sister, the heavenly Father, His Son, and the Holy Spirit are utterly and completely merciful. They know *all* about you, *all* you have ever done, and they are waiting with open arms to receive you into unending, boundless mercy. How can I say these things with such confidence? Because one day over eleven years ago, a cry for mercy changed my life forever.

THE DAY THE DEVIL ALMOST WON

It was wintertime and I had placed two-year-old David II in front of the television to watch *Sesame Street* beside his eight-month-old sister, Rebekah. Hoping my daughter would fall asleep, I placed Rebekah in the battery-operated swing and gave it a gentle push to get it started. Tears came to my eyes as I gave little David a coloring book and crayons and said, "Color this picture. Mommy will be right back."

But I had no intention of returning.

It was just a matter of finding our gun and walking into the marsh behind the house to pull the trigger. Life just wasn't worth living anymore.

After the birth of Rebekah, postpartum depression had come on full force. In addition exhaustion had taken its toll as night and day I was tormented by thoughts that I might somehow hurt my precious babies. Vowing that I would die before allowing those thoughts to become a reality, I was also bombarded by images of taking my own life. This day I was convinced that it was the only answer, the only way to put an end to the maddening thoughts.

Like the scene out of a movie, I made my way through the house in search of the gun. As I entered our lavishly decorated living room, the portrait of the children and me that was hanging on the wall grabbed my attention. We all looked so happy, so content, without a care in the world. Yet I could almost hear the smiling figures mocking me. The portrait, the room, the house—everything *looked* so perfect, but in reality, my life was a living hell. In answer to the mocking portrait I screamed, "It's a lie! It's *all* just a *lie!*" as I collapsed onto the floor in sobs.

A DESPERATE SEARCH FOR ANSWERS

Having been exposed to so much trauma and abuse as a child, I had been bound and determined to be a good mommy who would shield my children from all harm and danger, to the point that I became far too overprotective. But that was only one of the issues I was dealing with. Since so many years of my childhood had been blocked from my memory due to the extensive abuse, I had to read books to find out what childhood was supposed to be like. I had no clue. I also scoured book after book searching for how to be a good mother. The problem was, none of those books explained how a person like me—who did not ever remember feeling loved and safe—was to provide this loving and safe environment for her children. None of the books explained how I was to deal with the tormenting spirits that visited me nightly. Like the constant dripping of a leaky faucet, the continual thoughts had worn me down and convinced me that I was crazy, that I was losing my mind, and that I would eventually kill my family. Not one of the books even hinted at the answers that I so desperately needed.

I did not know it at the time, but there is only one book that has the power to drive away evil spirits and put an end to tormenting thoughts. That book is the Bible, and it is unlike any other book ever written. Its words are *alive!* When I did finally discovered this truth, I literally could not stop reading my Bible, for it contained all the answers I needed. I now know from personal experience that what Jesus said is true:

> **"And you shall know the truth, and the truth shall make you free."**
>
> **John 8:32**

That dreadful winter day, however, I did not know these things. My mind was absolutely consumed with terrifying images that until recently had only surfaced in nightmares. Having a baby girl had triggered memories of my own childhood. Over and over the scenes replayed in my mind of being molested by my then brother-in-law in the single-wide trailer on the family farm and being raped by him one summer while I was swimming in a nearby pond. None of the parenting books told me how I could put an end to this mental torment that robbed me of sleep night after night. For months I had grabbed Dave in the middle of the night, screaming through sobs, "Make it stop, Dave. *Please make it stop!*"

By this time, Dave was nearing the end of his rope too, as we say in the South. He had done all that he could possibly do to help me. He had sent me to therapists, hired a nanny, built me a new home, and granted my every wish from a natural standpoint. That winter day, however, none of the custom window treatments or the Mercedes in the garage could stop the torment I was experiencing. I know now that the mental illness was a result of all the years of molestation, rape, and religious abuse that I had never dealt with. The postpartum depression and exhaustion simply added sufficient stress to bring everything to a head. I could no longer suppress any of the emotions I had bottled up for so many years. Sadly the church I attended was no help at all. The leadership there basically told me to pick myself up by the bootstraps and do the best I could.

"Picking myself up" was no longer an option. Lying there on the rug in my living room—ironically named "Garden of Eden"—I screamed in despair, "Jesus, if You are who You say You are, then You can heal my mind! But if You are not, *You are the biggest fake I know!*"

About that time Dave arrived home from work and found me weeping uncontrollably, still on the floor. As he picked up my frail body writhing in sobs, I managed to utter, "Dave, you have two choices: You can either put me in a mental hospital or give me the .357 and clean me up in the marsh."

Oh, the grief that struck his face at that moment. The gravity of the situation and the realization that all of his efforts had failed suddenly sunk in. Now he, too, was in utter despair. But then he did a remarkable thing—he cried out to God. Remarkable because neither Dave nor I knew Him. We had attended church and appeared to be religious, but in reality, God was a total stranger to us. Nevertheless, from the depths of his soul Dave cried out, "Lord, have mercy on my wife! She cannot go on like this anymore."

Like a lightning bolt splitting the nighttime sky, those words literally ripped through the demonic darkness and went straight to the heart of God. As Dave's tears fell onto my face, all of a sudden a peace flooded my being that I had never known before. The crying ceased and for the longest time, we simply sat in silence, not wanting to move, not wanting the sacred moment to end. Something had changed and we both knew it. That night, for the first time in as long as I could remember, I slept peacefully.

MERCY TRIUMPHS OVER JUDGMENT

What we did not understand at the time, when Dave cried out for God to have mercy on me, it was equivalent to him praying that God would not allow judgment to fall upon me. The reality was that I deserved to die. My past included drugs, alcoholism (though cleverly hidden), extensive promiscuousness, jail, and more. Even though by this time in my life I had been "good" for a number of years, "being good" was not enough to save me and I knew it. Yes, the sexual abuse and being raised in a religious cult set me up for many of my sinful deeds, but the fact was, sin was sin and its penalty death. I simply could not stand up under the weight of the robe of judgment and criticism anymore, nor did I have any power to stop the onslaught of demonic attacks.

The thing I want to make clear here is the reason *why* I was so powerless. The answer is simple: *I was not God's child!* I was not a Christian. Of course the devil knew this, and he had taken full advantage of the many openings that sin had created in my life.

But now, when Dave called out for mercy, all of heaven came to attention. Even though I'm sure the devil tried to continue railing accusations against me before God, now Mercy said, *No! My mercy triumphs over judgment, and she will not die. She will live!* With that, the devil tucked his tail between his knees and whimpered away like the defeated foe he is.

A NEW DAY

That moment marked the single most pivotal moment of my life. James 2:13 confirms that "mercy triumphs over judgment" and my life is living proof. Things were set in motion that day and I have truly never been the same; almost immediately things began to change. I was able to stay home instead of checking into a mental hospital. Then my housekeeper, who had sensed for months that things were not as they seemed on the surface, introduced me to her sister who had been sexually abused as I had been. Jesus had healed and restored her, and her testimony gave me hope for the first time in my life that things could change for me. Imagine the impact of her assurances that Jesus would heal me and put my mind back together!

When I look back over that moment on the living room floor and see how the hand of God moved in my life, I still stand in awe. I wonder if in heaven one day I will get to see the replay of that moment and how the angels went to work immediately to set up my conversion and deliverance experience. Oh, how I love Jesus for removing the robe of judgment and criticism and replacing it with His mercy!

Although I did not know it back then, Jesus has been extending mercy to women in dire straights throughout eternity. Let's look at one instance recorded in John 8:

> **The scribes and Pharisees brought to Him a woman caught in adultery. And when they had set her in the midst, they said to Him, "Teacher, this woman was caught in adultery, in the very act. Now Moses, in the law, commanded us that such should be stoned. But what do You say?"**
>
> **vv. 3–5**

Although the Bible does not record the woman's thoughts, I imagine that like me, she was already throwing stones at herself emotionally. She knew what she had done. She knew it deserved judgment and death. The robe of judgment and criticism weighed heavily upon her as it did me.

Think about how shocked she must have been when she heard this esteemed Teacher, this holy Man of God, say,

> **"He who is without sin among you, let him throw a stone at her first."**
>
> **v. 7**

Imagine her disbelief as one by one these men turned and walked away! But she was not jumping for joy yet. *Now* she was standing alone before Jesus Himself. What on earth would He say? I can just picture her—head bowed, shoulders drawn forward in fear and shame.

Jesus, understanding her turmoil, slowly disarmed her.

> **"Woman, where are those accusers of yours? Has no one condemned you?"**
>
> **v. 10**

No doubt timidly, she replied, "No one, Lord."

> **And Jesus said to her, "Neither do I condemn you; go and sin no more."**
>
> **v. 11**

This makes me want to shout, *"Praise God!"* for I know the rush of emotions she must have experienced as the reality set in. The amazement ... the joy ... the relief. Oh, the relief! To no longer have the weight of judgment crushing the very life out of you!

My dear sister, I hope you are getting this, because this is what Jesus is saying to *you!* "I do not condemn you, I *love you!* Give Me that robe of judgment and criticism and let Me surround you with My mercy!"

BLESSED ARE THE MERCIFUL

The story of this adulterous woman and her accusers illustrates the natural tendency for humans to be judgmental. But the reality is, we *all* are like the *woman* in the story. Sin permeates the fiber of every human being, and the Bible confirms this:

> **All of us were like sheep that had wandered off.**
> **We had each gone our own way.**
>
> Isaiah 53:6 CEV

We all deserve death, but, praise God, that is not the end of the verse! Let's read the remainder of it:

> **But the Lord gave him** [Jesus] **the punishment we deserved.**

What motivated God to go to such lengths? I am convinced that it was His mercy! Mercy said, "No! My Son will take their judgment."

Now let's go back up to verse 5 to complete the picture:

> **He** [Jesus] **was wounded and crushed because of our sins; by taking our punishment, he made us completely well.**

The thing you must realize is that Mercy did this for *you!* Just like Jesus bore my judgment and made me completely well, He is inviting you to receive the same in your own life.

IT'S ALL BECAUSE OF MERCY

I have been a Christian and living a holy life for well over a decade now, but I know that I still have no right to judge others. I have learned that if there is anything good in you and me and if we have done anything of worth, it is only by the grace and mercy of God. The Holy Spirit is the One who gets the credit for opening my eyes to the wonder of Jesus and His Word. It was only after He revealed the loving, merciful, and kind nature of Jesus that I fell in love with the Savior. It is certainly nothing I can take credit for. If it had not been for mercy that day in my living room, I would not be a mom, a wife, and definitely not an evangelist of the Gospel of Jesus Christ. In fact, I would not be here at all. It was God's mercy that intervened and kept me from taking my own life. No, I cannot take credit for any of the good He has done in me or through me. It's all a result of His mercy. I just desire to be so "salty" that others will want to drink the living water as I have.

Not only have I *needed* a great deal of mercy, people tell me that I am unusually merciful toward others. The reason is that I am no longer wearing the robe of judgment and criticism. It does not take much for me to remember where I came from; and whenever I witness a prostitute, a homosexual, a drug addict, a gossip, a "mean" check-out clerk, a rude driver, a snob, or any other individual caught up in sin, what I really see is myself there on my living room floor, powerless to help myself. What I want people to know is that Jesus will meet them where they are and He will set them free just as He did me. No, I do not judge others in their sin. The only One qualified to judge is God Himself. In fact, Jesus issued the following warning:

> **"Judge not, that you be not judged. For with what judgment you judge, you will be judged; and with the measure you use, it will be measured back to you."**
>
> **Matthew 7:1–2**

I want to clarify one thing. When I say that I do not judge, it does not mean that I endorse sin or a sinful lifestyle because I do not. Mercy never winks at or condones sin. What it does mean is that I tell people that Jesus loves them and that He has a wonderful plan for their lives. Then I expect the Holy Spirit to go to work to open their eyes and change their hearts. We are only to plant seeds of love and the Good News when we can. Hopefully those seeds will bear fruit and these individuals will become born again. Then they can escape judgment for sin altogether!

One final thought about judgment and criticism. John 3:16 is a familiar verse about salvation, but verse 17 is not as widely known. Let's look at them together:

> **[Jesus said,] "For God so loved the world that He gave His only begotten Son, that whoever believes in Him should not perish but have everlasting life. For God did not send His Son into the world to condemn the world, but that the world through Him might be saved."**

What I want you to see here is that God does not win the lost by condemning them and neither will we. It is only when we are free of criticism and judgment and we are full of God's love that we can effectively minister the Gospel to the world. The truth is, God wants every single human on the planet to spend eternity with Him, and He uses us as His ambassadors to win them.

This week we are going to learn how the robe of criticism and judgment opens the door to self-righteousness. Then we are going to learn how to remove that robe and clothe ourselves in mercy. As you experience God's acceptance in a personal way, you will also begin to see others in a new light. Whereas at one time you might have had critical thoughts toward the unlovely and rejected, you will find your heart now welling up with compassion as you begin to see them through the eyes of Jesus. As you cry out for mercy on their behalf, all of heaven will come to attention and spiritual forces will be mobilized to deliver, help, and save.

Just leave the judging up to God. He can handle it.

Week 5

Take Off the Robes of Judgment and Criticism

Week 5, Day 1 — Recognizing the Robes

My dear sisters in Christ, the robes we are going to discard this week are ones most of us have and do not even realize it. Taking off these robes is a process to give us the freedom Jesus died to give us. Let's look at Isaiah 61:1-3 KJV together:

"The Spirit of the Lord God is upon me; because the Lord hath anointed me to preach good tidings unto the meek; he hath sent me to bind up the brokenhearted, to proclaim liberty to the captives, and the opening of the prison to them that are bound;

"To proclaim the acceptable year of the Lord, and the day of vengeance of our God; to comfort all that mourn;

"To appoint unto them that mourn in Zion, to give unto them beauty for ashes, the oil of joy for mourning, the garment of praise for the spirit of heaviness; that they might be called trees of righteousness, the planting of the Lord, that he might be glorified."

What were the five things Jesus came to do as prophesied by the Prophet Isaiah?

_____

_____

_____

_____

_____

_____

What is your definition of "criticism"?

_____

_____

_____

_____

Now, let's turn to *Vine's Expository Dictionary of New Testament Words* to see how the Greek definition of one of the Greek words trans-

111

lated "judgment" is defined. Part of the definition is a decision passed on the faults of others[6] and is cross-referenced to the word "condemnation."

What is your definition of the word "condemned"?

_____

_____

Once you realize this is the definition of these words, how does that make you feel?

_____

_____

_____

_____

Many times, especially we sisters in the Lord, can meet someone and size him or her up in about fifteen seconds. What if I told you that you do not have to do this any longer? You can just meet people and enjoy them and not pass judgment on their lives. The only question I find myself asking over and over when I meet people is whether or not they know Jesus. I used to be the "judgment queen" and could size up someone quickly and come up with a million excuses why I just did not like him or her or have a good feeling about that person. Do you know what that's called? SIN!

Write out Matthew 7:1-2:

_____

_____

_____

_____

_____

Let me illustrate, using the example of a precious woman who walked into my ministry office unexpectedly one Saturday afternoon. This woman was in her forties and had been an addict and a prostitute in order to get the drugs her body craved. There was a time in my life when I would not have been able to have pity on this woman. Now, I stopped and asked the Holy Spirit to have compassion through me and help me to listen to her story.

After a word of knowledge from God, she broke under the power of the Holy Spirit and it was revealed that she was severely abused as a child in ways I am not at liberty to share. She wept in my arms and I had the great opportunity to lead her to Jesus and see her meet her Savior.

---

[6]W. E. Vine, *An Expository Dictionary of New Testament Words* (Nashville, TN: Thomas Nelson, Publishers), 611.

It still amazes me that someone with my past can be given such an honor. You can stop reading and get up, as we of the Pentecostal faith do, and shout a little while over this story. At any rate, why do I tell you this story? Let's quit this "Pharisaical religion" and stop snubbing a world that needs Jesus. We have no reason not to offer these people the "living water" of the gospel and really leave the judging up to God Himself.

Relax as we begin this week and try not to judge anyone or decide you know more about their lives than God does. It always amazes me and deeply grieves me when I hear a Christian put down an addict or a prostitute. Let me say this loud and strong: *Except for the grace of God, you could be in the same shoes.* Pray for them, love them, and be a living Jesus to them.

Do you feel a need to unbutton the first button of these robes? Get those beautiful fingers ready to unbutton these ugly robes. We will talk again tomorrow. I love you dearly and am so proud of you for not letting the enemy of our souls make you quit this Bible study. You can see the end of the dressing room if you look closely and see your beautiful robe of righteousness waiting to be placed upon you, my beautiful sisters in Christ.

Week 5, Day 2 — The Woman at the Well — Part 1

The Holy Spirit directed my attention to a story in the Bible I have preached many times. It is the story of the Samaritan woman in John 4:1-26. Read this scripture in the Word, and by the end of today's lesson, you will see the parallel with the robes of judgment and criticism.

What does verse 4 say?

_____

_____

My sisters, the Holy Spirit needed to come into your life today and reveal two robes that are causing you to waste energy that you could be using to bless someone else's life. Let's believe that by the end of this week, when you meet someone for the first time, you will not allow your mind to question their integrity or social status or be suspicious about them in any way. Wouldn't this be wonderful? I am not in any way telling you to be naïve and just blindly trust people. You do not have to throw common sense out the window.

Write out John 2:23-25:

_____

_____

_____

I am trying to get across to you that you should get out of the negative mind-set of judging people's intentions or lives without permission. Lately, it seems all of the time that I am telling my children when they come home with stories of neighbors' children and their parents' reactions that this is NONE OF OUR BUSINESS. Raised with sexual abuse in my background, I tended to be a very nosey person and found myself critical of everyone. I praise Jesus that I have been delivered from all of my criticism and I can give people the truth of the gospel. It is their decision what to do with it. After I present them with the truth, I can know that God is their judge, not Jennifer Kostyal.

Now, back to our story in the book of John and the wonderful Samaritan woman.

There are four points to this story before we go any further.

1. Women in biblical times were considered greatly inferior to men. Within the Middle Eastern culture, a man was never allowed to speak to a woman in public. This meant a man would not even say hello to his sister, mother, or wife.

2. The Jewish people did not speak to the Samaritans. The Jews and Samaritans hated and avoided each other at all costs.

3. No self-respecting teacher or rabbi would ever speak to a woman with the reputation of the Samaritan woman.

4. Notice that the time of day this woman came to draw water from the well was noon. The girls and women of biblical times always went to the well early in the morning and in groups. This woman was a true social outcast.

Now, let's examine the Scriptures in more detail. Let's return to John, chapter 4.

What did Jesus ask the Samaritan woman?

_____

_____

_____

What was the Samaritan woman's response?

_____

_____

_____

Actually, this woman's comment was a racist comment in many ways and very critical. Here Jesus was offering this woman freedom and she was staring at both of their races. Now, my sweet sisters, do you mean to say racism is about judgment? Yes, racism is judgment and also a matter of pride. For someone to think one race is superior to another is judgment at its height. If you battle prejudice in any way, please stop this study, bow your head, and ask the Lord to forgive you and deliver you. We in the Body of Christ are not ever to look at race because our God is many colors and we are all made in His image and likeness.

Keep your fingers on John 4 and let's flip to one of my favorite verses, Romans 12:3.

In your own words, write what this verse is saying:

_____

_____

_____

_____

Back to the story of the Samaritan woman. Notice that when she gave Jesus the response about their races, He then told her she had no idea who was standing before her. Then she said, "Who do You think You are? You cannot hold a candle to Jacob who gave us this well!" (My paraphrase of what she said.)

When Jesus told her about this "living water," she thought she had discovered how never to thirst again and jumped at the chance to go into isolation. However, the Lord always desires two things for His girls. He wants to make sure we are in the Kingdom of God, and then He wants to heal us. Once He introduced her to the "living water," He then began to make her face her life so she could become free and tell others about Him.

Remember the saying, which I mentioned previously, "Hurting people hurt people"? When you are healed and whole, you will see no more need to prove yourself or judge others. You will have the heart to tell people about Jesus so they can be free.

We will come back to this story in John 4 tomorrow. Let's end today's study by saying a prayer of repentance for judging our sisters and brothers in Christ and the world.

Write your prayer of repentance for judging others and about removing the robes of judgment and criticism:

_____

_____

_____

_____

I love you and wish I could kneel beside you and give you a big hug. But most importantly, Jesus loves you and you are on your way to freedom. We will be unbuttoning more buttons tomorrow.

Week 5, Day 3 — The Samaritan Woman – Part 2

Before we finish with the Samaritan woman in John 4, I want to share a verse with you that can change your life. Remember, I am fanatical about the Word of God and will never tell you anything not backed up with the Word.

Read Matthew 22:37-40.

How can you tie these verses into taking off the robes of criticism and judgment?

_____

_____

_____

_____

Now, let's look at John 4:1-25. Answering the following questions:

What did Jesus ask the woman when she just wanted the "living water"? (v. 16).

_____

_____

What question did the woman ask Jesus after He told her all about her life? (v. 20).

_____

_____

When I read this scripture, my spirit went to the judging and criticizing we all have had to admit having. What this woman was asking Jesus is, "Who is correct, the Samaritans or the Jews, in how they worship?" Does this ring a bell in your thinking that one denomination is better than another?

Let me be real honest about a prejudice I have had toward the Southern Baptists due to the fact that the religious cult I was raised in hated this wonderful denomination and always made fun of their so-called "easy salvation." When the Lord delivered me out of the cult, I had been in it for thirty-one years, my husband Dave and I started fasting and praying over where we were to go to church. One day as I was riding through my neighborhood and had just finished a prayer, the Lord spoke very loudly to me as I rode by a local Baptist church and said, "HERE"! I was in a convertible and I looked up in the sky and said, "Me in a Baptist church?" The Lord repeated, "I said HERE!"

Because I was delivered and healed from so much abuse, I very much lined up with the Pentecostals in my loud worship and shouting to the Lord. However, I went home and found that the Lord had been telling Dave the same thing. So we went to the very next service they had and I felt very much at home. This church truly blessed me and for six years gave me a grounding in the basic principles of faith in Christ that I had never experienced before. I became best friends with the Senior Pastor's wife and adore her to this day.

Dave and I met some of the nicest and most godly people within this Southern Baptist church that, to this day, are very close friends. Some even travel with us in our ministry. All of my immediate family were born again at this church, and this church will always hold a special place in my heart.

We need to stop our judgment and criticism of all denominations and love everyone in the Body of Christ and rejoice with their success in the Lord. Repent of your prejudices and keep the Word of God as your plumb line and worship Jesus. It truly will not matter if you are Baptist, Pentecostal, Charismatic, Catholic, Lutheran, or any other denomination.

What did Jesus say in verse 23 that will make us throw off our judgment robes of denominations?

_____

_____

What truth did this "outcast" have that she spoke of in verse 25?

_____

_____

This is such an exciting thing when Jesus tells this woman He is the Messiah. All theologians agree that Jesus first revealed He was the Messiah to this woman. Did you hear this? Jesus went out of His way to a despicable, five-times divorced woman and told her He was the Messiah. Jesus is our example, and if He went out of His way to love the unlovable, we need to throw aside our robes of judgment and witness to this sinful world! Once we love them and tell them about our Jesus, they will go and tell others that the Messiah has come and that we need to get prepared for His second coming.

Now that the Lord has opened up so many doors for me to hear the personal testimonies of great women and men of God, it always seems that it is the most rejected who have the most powerful anointing on their lives. I find that those who are the most powerful speakers and preachers are those who realize that, had it not been for Jesus, they would have nothing. Without a doubt, we will shout it from the rooftops and love all who cross our path when we realize that Jesus is the Son of God and that, through His death, burial, and resurrection, we are made free.

We will talk more tomorrow about our new friend, the Samaritan woman, and get ready to throw these ugly robes of criticism and judgment in the trash in Jesus' name. Stop being critical of yourselves too. You are my sisters and I love you.

Week 5, Day 4 — Full of Love!

I was so excited about writing this day of your Bible study. It is before 6:00 a.m. and it is still dark outside. Today, we will witness a great change in the life of the Samaritan woman that truly shows how taking off the robes of criticism and judgment will set you free to love even those who have despised you.

When we do a deep study of the Word of God, we find that we are becoming more and more like Jesus. Let's open our Bibles to John 4:27-42 and answer the following questions:

What did the Samaritan woman do when she realized Jesus was the Messiah?

_____

_____

_____

_____

Why was this so significant due to her past history with this city?

_____

_____

_____

_____

Isn't it beautiful that this woman went back into the town where she was so rejected and witnessed about a man who told her about her life? Also, what is so amazing is that she was anointed of God to do so in such a manner that the entire town came out and saw Jesus. She received and believed in the "Living Word" and began to tell a town that had shunned and despised her that they could have this "living water" from Jesus.

When we look into the eyes of Jesus and truly realize that He is the Messiah, all of our hatred, prejudices, bitterness, judgment, and criticism will melt and we will find ourselves just talking about our Savior.

Read John 4:34-38.

What was Jesus' food?

_____

_____

What does Jesus say about the harvest?

_____

_____

My sisters, the fields around you are truly ripe for harvest. There are so many hurting people who need to know the love of Jesus. You are a laborer once you meet Jesus and are anointed to tell the world that, yes, Jesus is the Son of God! This woman had every reason to just go home and revel in the fact that she was whole and at peace. However, she could not contain the joy of knowing the One who was the Messiah.

I will never forget when I realized Jesus was the Son of God and that He had, in fact, forgiven me of all of my sins and healed my mind. I danced and shouted around my house with my son David who was three at the time. My husband cried tears of joy as he watched a wife who previously could hardly function sing and dance and proclaim, "Dave, I am healed in the name of Jesus!"

What is amazing is that this was eleven years ago (at the time of this writing) and today I am even more excited and want to do more for my Lord. You see, my sweet sisters, when you are healed and made whole, rejection by people no longer affects you but causes you to share truth and joy and pray for them who wish to reject you. Go ahead, like the Samaritan woman did and talk with Jesus and ask Him if He is, in fact, the Messiah of the world if you are not absolutely sure of this fact. Sit with Him at the "well in your house" and tell Him about all of your pain and the reason you find yourself judging and criticizing. Then, ask Him to take these heavy robes off of you so you can be free.

I feel that this woman had many conversations with Jesus after her deliverance, and I know she was always grateful for all He had done in her life. She went from a "nobody" to a woman who affected an entire town.

Get free, my sisters, in the name of Jesus and let people see the new, free, and wonderful you! You will be amazed how much your family and friends will appreciate the NEW YOU IN JESUS. My family was amazed at the change. This affected my husband so tremendously that he is in charge of the business portion of our ministry and knows Jesus can make you whole!

We have had many people in our home that people in the church would probably be scared to have in theirs, but I am like the Samaritan woman. However, with my past, I would have been scared of me too before Jesus came into my life. In fact, I was scared of me!

Do you feel the robes coming off of you as you look in Jesus' eyes and just accept His love for you? Can't you feel it falling off of you as you decide to love the world and your sisters in Christ? Isn't it nice to not be full of pride and think that you have all of the answers? Isn't it wonderful to just relax and know that ONLY JESUS truly has the answers and that He has told us to love our God and love our neighbors as ourselves?

Wow! What a joy to get rid of these robes and be able to move our shoulders and feel the freedom of not having these heavy robes that caused us to use a great deal of energy the wrong way!

Tomorrow we will discuss some scriptures that will finalize this week's study. Remember John 8:31-32: **"Then Jesus said to those Jews who believed Him, 'If you abide in My word, you are My disciples indeed. And you shall know the truth, and the truth shall make you free.'"**

Week 5, Day 5 — Let's Have Grace!

When I wrote this week's lesson, the Holy Spirit reminded me what the number five means. It means "grace."

Write your own definition of "grace":

_____

_____

The *Holman Bible Dictionary* defines "grace" as follows: Undeserved acceptance and love received from another, especially the characteristic attitude of God in providing salvation for sinners. For Christians, the word "grace" is virtually synonymous with the gospel of God's gift of unmerited salvation in Jesus Christ.[7]

Looking at this definition, we have to be real with each other and realize we did absolutely nothing to make Jesus die for us on Calvary. Therefore, we must realize we get no credit for what happened thousands of years before we were even born!

Get rid of all pride which is the root of judgment, and love and accept everyone and enjoy the freedom of such a life. Relax and be at peace, because the removal of these robes in my life was one of the most liberating things to experience, and I know in my spirit you are experiencing the same joy as you finally take them off and let the real you be revealed and just love your sisters and brothers in Christ. Hallelujah to the Lamb of God!

Now, don't you see the need to extend grace to our brothers and sisters in Christ and stop judging or criticizing them? Galatians 6:7 says,

[7]*Holman's Bible Dictionary*, 573.

"Whatever a man [woman] sows, that he [she] will also reap."
Let's sow grace and love each other as Christ loved us. Now, let's move
on to some more scriptures that show us the need to not let the robes
of judging and criticism ever become a part of our person again.

Write out Romans 14:4:

_____

_____

_____

_____

Write out 1 Corinthians 11:28:

_____

_____

Within the Word of God, we are told to judge ourselves, not others.
When we look at Paul's instructions to the Corinthian church, we see
him explaining how we are to examine our lives before we partake of
the Lord's Supper. Now, we are not to be looking around and telling
anyone who has or has not the right to partake of the Lord's Supper.
We would not even dare to do so. However, we are doing the same thing
when we pass judgment on someone's life in other situations.

We are known by our fruits, the Lord tells us, and our lives speak
of the love of Christ and whether or not we are obeying the Word of
God. However, we are to examine ourselves. Be at peace as these robes
are finally removed. By spending a week telling you not to judge others, I am in no way telling you to affirm sin. The Word of God is my
judge and the only judge in any of our lives as Christians.

**Write a prayer to the Lord for the gratitude you feel in your
heart, knowing you can relax and stop judging and criticizing others:**

_____

_____

_____

_____

_____

I am very proud of you and know you will feel so much lighter now.
Next week we will take off our final robe that I find everyone on the
face of the earth has dealt with, and that is the robe of REJECTION.

I love you!

Will He Really Love Me?

Now a certain woman had a flow of blood for twelve years,
and had suffered many things from many physicians. She had spent
all that she had and was no better, but rather grew worse.
Mark 5:25–26

I was terrified to tell Dave about the awful things I had done—and that had been done to me—over the twenty-six years leading up to our wedding day. The years of sexual abuse had stolen my virginity at such a young age, and I did not have the courage to tell him that I had been raped at age nine by one of the guests coming to our wedding. The robe of rejection paralyzed me.

Nevertheless, the big day finally arrived. But what should have been one of the happiest days of my life was overshadowed by guilt and shame. There I stood next to my biological father in the foyer of this magnificent church, wearing an exquisite white wedding gown. No one had to tell me that white wasn't my color. But Dave nor I had been married before, and I knew that his Catholic family desired for their son to be met by his bride wearing white. He certainly deserved it, for he had maintained his purity.

From all outward appearance, everything was picture perfect. The large Catholic church, elegantly decorated and packed with hundreds of well-wishers, provided a surreal backdrop to this fairy-tale romance. Yet instead of identifying with Cinderella as she married her prince, I was certain that I belonged in the ashes, like a rejected stepchild. Saddest of all was that part of me dreaded our honeymoon night and once again having to face the awful truth about myself. How could I possibly don the white-as-snow bridal lingerie awaiting me in our suite?

Dave had waited for over a year to take me into his arms as Mrs. David M. Kostyal, and although he knew I was not a virgin, he had no idea of all the deeds I had been a part of during my lifetime. All he wanted was for everything to be perfect for us as we began our new life together as man and wife.

THE UGLY TRUTH

That night, as I stood in the beautiful marble bathroom of our honeymoon suite, I almost fainted as I caught a glimpse of myself in the mirror. The robe of rejection had cruelly distorted the image, like one of those peculiar mirrors at the fair. All I could see was a pitiful girl covered with filth from perverse hands and acts that I had been a part of for over ten years of my life, beginning when I was very young. What a time to envision those horrific scenes in my mind as I was getting ready to be with my husband for the first time. Dave did not deserve this kind of wife. Part of me wanted to run, but I had made a vow on that altar that I was determined to keep. I kept telling myself that I would be a good wife no matter how "unclean" I felt on the inside.

That night after consummating our marriage, Dave slept peacefully beside "the woman of his dreams." But sleep eluded me, due to the "truth" I had withheld from my precious husband. When I was sure that Dave was fast asleep, I quietly climbed out of bed and walked over to the honeymoon basket provided for us by the hotel. I was looking for something in particular—something I had turned to many times to deaden the thoughts of my past—alcohol. I then proceeded to drink the entire bottle of champagne. Before passing out, I carefully deposited the empty carafe in the hallway, hoping a hotel employee would pick it up before morning. Dave never found out till years later when I confessed.

Amazingly, I was up and about early the next morning, greeting my husband and the brisk Charleston air without even the slightest hangover. You see, I had turned to alcohol for many years to self-medicate the festering wounds deep within me and had mastered its side effects. What was I doing drinking champagne alone on my honeymoon? I was desperately trying to drown out the fact that this wonderful man had married an "unclean" woman.

A WOMAN OF UNCOMMON COURAGE

The Bible speaks of another unclean woman. Mark 5 tells us that for twelve long years this poor lady had suffered from an incurable blood flow and had endured as many unpleasant treatments as her meager finances would allow. Now, at the end of her rope, her savings totally depleted, she was no better and had actually grown worse.

As a last resort, she decided to seek out a Healer whom she had heard much about. Having exhausted every natural means, she knew that the supernatural healing power of God was her only hope. Yet how could she ever get near Him? She was a marked woman. The hemorrhaging had caused her to be shunned by society and declared unclean, preventing her from being able to participate in communal feasts and sacrifices like the other women in the community. People avoided her like the plague. How would she ever press her way through the crowd without being recognized?

Then another obstacle—Jesus was surrounded by a multitude of people. Did she even have the strength to endure the pushing and shoving of the throng?

No doubt the thought also hit her: *This is a holy man. What if I defile Him?* She would have to use the utmost caution so as not to be detected. She would be discreet—"If only I may touch His clothes, I shall be made well" (v. 28.) Then, continuing to blend in with the crowd, she would quietly make her way home, not disturbing anyone.

It was risky, but this was her last shot. She had to try. Besides, what could be worse than the pain and suffering she had already endured? So, propelled by the dream in her heart and armed with uncommon courage, this woman launched into her covert mission.

What she didn't know was that another person—a prominent synagogue leader named Jairus—had set out on a similar mission to save his dying daughter, and their destinies were about to collide.

Jairus reached Jesus first. Falling to his knees, he begged the Healer earnestly, "My little daughter lies at the point of death. Come and lay Your hands on her, that she may be healed, and she will live" (v. 23).

Responding to the man's faith, Jesus turned to go with Jairus, the multitude still thronging. All the while, the nameless woman was slowly making her way to the Master.

There! she must have cried out in her heart when she finally made contact. She barely touched the hem, but it was enough. Immediately power surged throughout her being and she knew that she had been made whole.

But she wasn't the only one who recognized that something significant had taken place. Suddenly, stopping in His tracks, Jesus asked, "Who touched My clothes?" (v. 30).

Imagine how the words must have stunned her, the clash of emotions that must have erupted within her. In a moment's time, she went from total elation over being healed to devastation that she was about to be betrayed. Hadn't she already suffered enough rejection? Now she was going to be exposed in front of everyone.

A STUNNING PROCLAMATION

Yes, she was about to be exposed, but for much different reasons than she anticipated. I believe that Jesus already knew the answer to His question and that He had a very definite purpose in asking it. Verse 32 says, "He looked around to see *her* who had done this thing" (emphasis added). Not just any old someone. Jesus knew that *she* had touched Him. He knew that this woman had stepped out of her comfort zone and gone to great lengths to partake of His anointing. It makes me smile when I see the great heart of love that Jesus has toward "His girls."

This outcast woman wanted desperately to remain anonymous, but Jesus had other plans. He desired to honor her before them all:

"Daughter, your faith has made you well. Go in peace, and be healed of your affliction."

v. 34

In those two brief sentences, Jesus did three things that absolutely rocked the community:

- He announced to everyone—including this well-known leader of the synagogue—that this "unclean woman" was His *daughter*.

- He pointed to *her* example to set the bar for great faith.

●· And most shocking of all, He announced to the world that He—the spotless Lamb of God—was not corrupted by her touch, but rather she was cleansed by Him!

Imagine the shock to Jairus, who because of his position had most likely prevented this woman from entering the temple due to her condition. Imagine his fury when in this midst of this "interruption," messengers arrived to announce that his daughter had died! *Couldn't this woman have waited? Didn't Jesus know that there was no time to lose? And now He's too late!* Of course Jesus went on to raise Jairus' daughter from the dead, but as amazing as that miracle was, it was Jesus' interaction with this unnamed woman He called daughter that so touches my heart.

I KNOW HOW SHE FELT

Although the cause of our uncleanness differed, I have a pretty good idea how the hemorrhaging woman felt when she realized she had been made whole. Now, almost sixteen years after that night of our honeymoon, Dave is no longer married to an "unclean" woman, for since then, I have come to know the truth. In fact, according to the Word of God, Dave has never been with an "unclean woman" because the blood of Jesus has washed away all of my sins as well as those committed against me. According to the Word of God, they have been removed as far as the east is from the west and my heavenly Father doesn't even remember them! (See Ps. 103:12; Isa. 43:25.)

These truths have revolutionized my life and the way I view myself. Just as there was no part of my life that the abuse did not affect, the Good News of Jesus has permeated every fiber of my being. I'm simply not the woman I once was. And He will do the same for you. Jesus offers this great hope to anyone who calls upon Him, and that is why I gladly share my story. No matter how badly you have been rejected or abused, no matter what you may have done to be "unclean" in the world's eyes, when you meet Jesus, you are beautifully transformed from the inside out. He says, "Though your sins are like scarlet, they shall be as white as snow," (Isa. 1:18) as His blood cleanses you through and through. Becoming a Christian enables you to hold your head high knowing "your Daddy" is exceedingly proud of you. He removes the robe of rejection once and for all and covers You with the cloak of His love.

You may be wondering how Dave reacted when he finally learned the full truth about my life. In short, all of my fears were unfounded and God's love prevailed. Like Jesus, Dave saw my heart and loved the real me. He simply wanted me to be well and whole, and he faithfully stood by me as I walked out my healing. You see, God's love is far superior to man's love alone. The apostle Paul describes this love in one of his letters to the Corinthians:

[God's love] ... rejoices when right and truth prevail. Love bears up under anything and everything that comes, is ever ready to believe the best of every person, its hopes are fadeless under all circumstances, and it

endures everything [without weakening]. Love never fails.

1 Corinthians 13:6–8 AMP

God's love transformed our lives and took our marriage to an even higher level than before. Together we discovered the truth from God's Word, and just as Jesus promised, that truth has set us free. That awful robe of rejection is forever a thing of the past.

FURTHER REVELATION

I would like to return to our story about the woman with the issue of blood for a moment. The Lord has revealed some additional nuggets of truth that have thoroughly blessed me, and I would like to share them with you. Let's look again what Jesus said to the woman:

"Daughter, your faith has made you well. Go in peace, and be healed of your affliction."

Mark 5:34

Referring to the fact that Jesus chose to use the word "Daughter" when addressing the woman, biblical scholars agree that there is no other instance in the Word of God where He uses such a term of endearment. What a precious way for our Lord to honor her. I personally believe that this is the term He also uses to describe you and me. Close your eyes and hear Him say it to you: *Daughter.* That's right—*Daughter.*

You, my sweet sister, are His very precious daughter.

Another fascinating aspect in the Lord's statement is in regard to the Greek word translated "healed" in this passage: *sozo.* According to *Strong's Exhaustive Concordance, sozo* comes a primary word meaning "safe." It means—among other things—to save, deliver, protect, heal, preserve, and make whole. In other words, *sozo* includes healing of the whole person. In the case of the woman with the issue of blood, every facet of her life was made whole the moment she touched Jesus. Verse 30 says that "power" went out of Him. Can you imagine what it felt like as this power surged through her being? More importantly, did you know that this same power is available to heal—*sozo*—you today? Just like the woman with the issue of blood, when we reach out to Jesus as our Lord and Savior, He immediate stops what He is doing and looks us in the eyes, saying, "What do you need today, My sweet, precious daughter?" In His arms we are safe.

THE PROBLEM IS GLOBAL

The story of this woman makes me smile, but in my heart I cry at the same time. Why? Because women all around the world are hemorrhaging in their souls. Silently they have endured ever conceivable kind of abuse and rejection, and it seems no one has taken the time to notice. Usually these women try to deaden the pain and patch themselves up the best way they know how, but most have given up hope that they can ever be truly free. Depending on the degree of their hemorrhaging, these women may become prostitutes, drug addicts, shopa-holics, workaholics, or some other "holic," in an attempt to quell the pain of their tortured souls. Some, in order to prevent further abuse by men, turn to homosexuality. Others turn to academia to fill the void. Some, in an effort to elevate themselves in the eyes of others, snob-bishly look down on the less fortunate. All build walls to protect them-selves from experiencing further pain.

Amazingly, many women know that something is not right inside, yet they do not know what or why. They only know they feel unclean, flawed, defective. Women are masters at covering up their pain and hiding their abuse, but deep down they feel powerless to clean up the filth that never goes away. I find that all forms of abuse make the vic-tim feel inadequate. Until they reach out for help, most women isolate themselves more and more, till eventually some quit trying at all to be accepted. In extreme cases, some women have to be institutionalized. Some go as far as to take their own lives.

If they only knew ... Jesus is waiting with open arms.

What about You?

As if the internal torment weren't enough, to be shunned like the woman in our story is the lot of millions of women. Perhaps you can relate. These women know that they are not supposed to go to certain places or do certain things because of their "condition." *Why try to find a godly man, when I am so undeserving? Why go to church where every-one there knows the filthy things I have done? Why try to fit in when everyone knows my family history? Why try? Why?*

It only takes one look from a "respectable" person (in society's eyes) to remind these women of their "proper place." "Your kind doesn't belong here" can be said without a single word being uttered. But do not be fooled. *Everyone* has at least one skeleton in his or her closet making every living soul unclean and unwhole. Never think for a minute that you are alone, my sweet sister. It is the human condition until a person is washed clean by Jesus.

Oh, to look back and remember the many times that I felt more wel-come in a bar than a church pew. But today, thanks to my Jesus, I can go to any church anywhere and know I am loved by the Jesus the rest are singing about. I know Him personally.

Dear sister, I want you to hear me on this. You are important to the Lord Jesus and He will literally come to a complete halt if you will but cry out to Him. Have courage and press in. He is the answer You have been searching for. Let Him look you in the eyes and shower His love upon you. You may not be able to physically touch the hem of His gar-ment, but you can touch Him through His Word. You can touch Him in prayer. And He will touch your heart.

When at first you realize you have His attention, don't turn and run away. Look Him in the eyes and pay close attention as He says, *Daughter, I love you. I will never reject you. You are My sweet girl for whom I died.*

When I realized that Jesus was truly the Messiah and He cleaned me up, I was amazed that I no longer cared what people thought of me. *Jesus* loved me. He washed me clean of the molestation, rape, and all of the things done to me by men. I was able to forgive the "religious" people who thought of me as "trash." When I knew I had Jesus' attention, it no longer mattered what the rich, the poor, the beautiful, or the famous thought. I had the King's favor. Finally, I was okay! You see, this is why I do not mind telling my story to whoever will listen. My story is simply an extension of *His* story, and every time I share it, it reminds the devil of his total defeat at the resurrection. Jesus overcame him, and now I overcome him the blood of the Lamb and the word of my testimony. (Rev. 12:11.)

Jesus will never reject you, dear sister. You are getting ready to learn this week that you serve an infinitely wonderful God who loves you more than your mind can conceive. Jesus lights up the sky nightly, putting on a fireworks display to announce His adoration to you—"His precious girl."

Now I am going to share a couple of verses with you, and I want you to let them sink deep into your spirit and soul. You are His daughter and it does not matter what any person has ever done or said to you, you are His treasure. Jesus gave up heaven for you and desires to lavish you with His love.

You are a people set apart as holy to God, your God. God, your God, chose you out of all the people on Earth for himself as a cherished, personal treasure.

Deuteronomy 7:6 MSG

"For the Lord your God has arrived to live among you. He is a mighty Savior. He will give you victory. He will rejoice over you with great gladness; he will love you and not accuse you." Is that a joyous choir I hear? No, it is the Lord Himself exulting over you in happy song.

"I have gathered your wounded and taken away your reproach."

Zephaniah 3:18 TLB

Dear sweet sister, bask in His love today and know that He has made you whole and clean. You are amazingly beautiful to the only One who matters—Jesus Christ, your Lord.

Week 6

Take Off the Robe of Rejection

Week 6, Day 1 — Rejection

My dear, precious sisters in Christ, this is the final week for us to remove a robe that ALL of us have been affected by or have worn many times. I am so proud of you and know you feel lighter; however, the battle is not over. This week, remain in prayer and in the Word and you will see the final victory come forth in the name of Jesus.

We will begin today to remove the robe of rejection and never allow this extremely heavy and damaging garment to resist the power of the blood of Jesus. I say loudly to you, the Lord Jesus truly loves you and He will never reject you! Did you hear the words I just said? The Lord will never reject you! This is so wonderful for me to be able to write this study and know without a doubt that these words are true. This alone makes me want to bow my head and say, "Thank You, Jesus, for never rejecting me. I will love You forever, and I can't wait to tell You in heaven that Your love is what helped me make it through this life on earth.

In your own words, write out your definition of "to reject":

_____

_____

According to *Merriam-Webster's Collegiate Dictionary,* the definition of "reject" is to cast off; to refuse to hear, receive, or admit; not wanted, unsatisfactory, or not fulfilling standard requirements.[8]

Let's begin today's lesson by getting into the Word immediately.

Write out Deuteronomy 4:31:

_____

_____

_____

_____

Write out Joshua 1:5:

_____

_____

_____

[8]*Merriam-Webster's Collegiate Dictionary*, 11th Ed. (Springfield, MA: Merriam-Webster, Inc., 2004), 1050.

Write out John 14:18:

_____

_____

_____

_____

_____

Write out 2 Corinthians 4:9:

_____

_____

_____

_____

My sisters, I wanted you to get an understanding that Jesus loves you and could not and would not reject or forsake you. It is so important that you understand that you cannot stop Jesus from loving you and that His love is unconditional and forever! All day today, I want you to tell yourself, "Jesus loves me and that will never change." Daughters of God, from the foundations of the earth Jesus knew that He would die for you and He did.

As you have heard me say, I was rejected at age thirty because I became a believer in Jesus Christ, and my parents and all my sisters and my brother in the natural disowned me. I thought I would die. The only way I could deal with it was to get up very early in the morning and read the Word of God over and over out loud and tell myself that Jesus loved me and would never leave me or forsake me.

I will never forget when a brother in Christ called me very early one morning to tell me about Mark 10:29. This verse says that when we give up our earthly family and property for the gospel's sake, we will gain a hundredfold in this present age and in the age to come eternal life for all we have sacrificed for the gospel. This verse means so much to me, and I have lived it for over ten years now.

Today I literally have so many moms, dads, brothers, and sisters in Christ that I have lost count. I used to cry out to the Lord, however, to send me some parents. He did just that when I was spiritually adopted by Rev. Roy Belon and Elder Velma Belon of Chapel Hill, North Carolina. They have been such good parents to me and wonderful grandparents to my children. I love introducing them at our conferences, because it is such a testimony of the goodness of the Lord. Also, my adopted mom and dad are of the black race and I am a white woman, so what a testimony when David II and Rebekah introduce their grandparents to their friends. God is so good! He is a God of many colors.

Jesus said His family consisted of those who did the will of the Father. This is true for me as well. It is the reason I can tell you that you are my sisters and I love you very much.

Since becoming a minister, I have heard many rejection stories that have brought tears to my eyes. I always have the same response to my dear sisters as I hold them in my arms: "Jesus loves you and He will never hurt you. Just rest in His arms."

Let's end today's lesson by looking at one of my favorite scriptures about the love of our Daddy in heaven: **"For I am persuaded that neither death nor life, nor angels nor principalities nor powers, nor things present nor things to come, nor height nor depth, nor any other created thing, shall be able to separate us from the love of God, which is in Christ Jesus our Lord"** (Romans 8:38-39).

Sisters, there is absolutely nothing that can separate you from Jesus. He loves you so much and He will forever. Receive His love and be at peace.

Week 6, Day 2 — You Are Not Forsaken

In today's society there are so many women and children who are being forsaken and rejected by their families. Many times in my office I hold a beautiful woman who has found out her husband has left her for another woman after many dedicated years of marriage. You would think the moans and groans were because they had just heard some loved one had died. It is the most humbling experience to hold someone who is in this kind of pain.

My dear sisters in Christ, rejection of this kind feels like hearing of the death of a loved one. One day a man you gave children to, along with the youth of your life, decides that, because of the enemy dangling a carrot called adultery in his face, he will walk out of your life and never look back. This kind of pain is truly indescribable. Many times I have held the children left behind in divorce and heard them say, "I miss my daddy. Why has he left me?"

What both the mom and the children are screaming from the depth of their very being is, "How could someone I trusted and loved reject me this way?" The damage done is so deep that only the blood of Jesus can heal it.

As I write this lesson, I am reminded where the Prophet Jeremiah speaks of the balm of Gilead. (Jeremiah 8:22.) My dear sisters, this balm of Gilead represents the Word of the Lord. This is a balm that can heal the deepest wounds in your life and allow you to have hope again. How can I make such a claim and know without a doubt there is a balm in Gilead? It is because I was greatly wounded and the Word of God healed me and delivered me, leaving me whole in the beautiful name of Jesus.

According to *Holman's Bible Dictionary,* here is an interesting fact about the balm of Gilead: Gilead was famous, especially for its flocks and herds, and also for the balm of Gilead, an aromatic and medicinal preparation, probably derived from the resin of a small balsam tree."[9]

I have been drawn to this balm many times over the past decade of my life and have found in my research that this balm also had beautifying qualities. This balm will make everything it touches more beautiful by showing us who we are in Jesus. The Word of God will affect every aspect of our being. Whenever we take the Word of God and start applying it to our lives, we will be amazed at the healing qualities it possesses. Let's go to the Word of God and receive some "balm of truth."

Write out Psalm 119:107:

_____

_____

Write out Psalm 119:89:

_____

_____

_____

Write out Psalm 91:14:

_____

_____

_____

There are so many scriptures in which King David wrote about the love of God and the Word of God being more precious to him than anything else in the world. King David understood rejection at the highest level. As you read back over his life, you will see that when the Prophet Samuel came to his father Jesse's house, Jesse did not even mention David to the prophet. David was an afterthought to his own earthly dad, but he became the next king of Israel to his heavenly Father.

You are not what man thinks of you, my sisters. You are daughters of the King of kings and the Lord of lords.

Also, our Lord and Savior, Jesus, understood rejection more than anyone who has ever lived on this earth. My dear sisters, a trick of the enemy is to tell you that there is no one else on the face of the earth who has gone through what you are going through. I used to say over and over again, "Lord, please show me someone who has been completely disowned by his mother and father." I used to cry out for someone to relate to. Praise God! I found that King David can relate. (Psalm 27:10.)

[9]*Holman's Bible Dictionary,* 554.

Listen to me, my sweet sisters in Christ, you are covered in the shadow of the wings of God according to Psalm 91. You are loved with an everlasting love, and your Daddy in heaven will NEVER LEAVE YOU OR FORSAKE YOU. Even if everything in your life seems to be spinning out of control, look to the hills from whence comes your strength.

Many times I have had to just lie prostrate on the floor and cry until there were no more tears and tell my Daddy in heaven to please help me or I would not make it. One morning in particular, I was weeping over the disowning by my biological mother. I felt I was physically dying, knowing I was raising her grandchildren whom she had not seen in a few years and whose childhood was slipping away. I had asked the Lord how a mother could disown her child, and I asked Him to heal me of this great affliction.

I sat in my breakfast area and asked Him to please give me strength. I opened my Bible and it fell open to Isaiah 49:15-16. I wept for hours, thanking my God for loving me and reminding me that He would never leave me or forsake me.

Isaiah 49:15-16 says, **"Can a woman forget her nursing child, and not have compassion on the son of her womb? Surely they may forget, yet I will not forget you. See, I have inscribed you on the palms of My hands; your walls are continually before Me."**

Rest, my sweet sisters, in the arms of the One who loved you enough to die for you and pay the penalty for every wrong ever done to you. You are so loved and adored by the Creator of the universe. Take time today to hear His voice. I assure you, He will say, "I love you and I will never leave you or reject you." We will talk again tomorrow.

Week 6, Day 3 — You Are Loved!

Many times when my children were young, they would get up on my lap, look me in the eyes, and say with such beautiful voices, "I love you, Mommy." Wow! Words cannot describe the feeling that comes over you when such pure love is poured into your heart.

Dear sisters, our Father God, or as I like to call Him, Daddy, loves it when we take time out of our day and say, "I love You, Daddy." Those words bring Him so much joy and make Him smile big enough to light up the night sky with beautiful firework displays of His love towards us, His girls. I love saying, "Daddy loves His girls and He will not stop until He sees us made whole and protected."

Many times when we are rejected, we carry this deep wound within us and act out this pain without realizing what is causing us to do the things we do. I find many times rejection affects women by causing addiction to drugs or alcohol. Praise Jesus for Christians in the field of psychiatry who are called to help the children of God. However, I know

133

what rejection does to the human soul and the deep damage one feels from any form of rejection or abandonment. I also know the healing power from the blood of Jesus!

In yesterday's lesson, I shared about crying out to the Lord to give me someone to relate to who had been rejected by his or her mother or father. After I had cried out, the Lord directed a dear friend of mine to tell me about Psalm 27:10: **"When my father and my mother forsake me, then the Lord will take care of me."** *The Amplified Version* reads, **"Although my father and my mother have forsaken me, yet the Lord will take me up [adopt me as His child]."**

When the Lord revealed this verse to me, it totally changed how I viewed the disowning of my family due to the fact that a great king named David had walked the walk I was walking and had learned much through his rejection of man. I always say, "If you find someone highly anointed and in love with Jesus, it is because they have suffered and learned to rely totally on the Lord."

The Holy Spirit started changing me and showing me that I could truly do all things through Jesus Christ who strengthens me, and showing me how to depend on His love to see me through the days of loneliness and confusion. The Word of God truly was more important than the food I ate. It helped me to get through the loneliest days of my life.

When we left my parents' church, I did not have any friends outside of my extended family and it was so scary. However, the Lord sent us to a great church in our community and put favor on my life. I ended up teaching the women's group there and sharing my testimony. It was not easy because I had never been outside of the comfort zone of a church of twenty to thirty people where the majority of the members were kin to me. The Lord opened up a new world to me and showed me wonderful things as He walked by my side and continuously showed me with His Word that He was with me and would never leave me or forsake me.

Let's look at some verses and once again get some more Word into us so we can continue to change and be set free by the Word of God. Hallelujah!

Write out Psalm 27:1:

_____

_____

Write out Psalm 9:9-10:

_____

_____

_____

_____

Write out Psalm 22:10:

_____

_____

My dear sisters, listen closely. It does not matter who has rejected you. The most important person in the world, Jesus, will never reject you. He is present when we mess up and He still says, "I love you and I want to pick you up and place you back on the path of joy and peace."

Not many of us have ever experienced unconditional love, so this is a new concept for us in many ways. The idea of someone loving us and not wanting something in return is very new for us. However, our Father God just wants us to know that He loves us and wants us to love Him.

Did you know that you were created for God's pleasure? He truly looks at us play and work in the Kingdom and gets such joy from us. It was such a new concept for me to grasp that my Lord and my God just enjoyed me and truly wanted to spend time with me, His daughter. Do you see how special you really are? You are such a pleasure for the God of the universe, and when He looks at you, He just smiles and says, "There are My girls!"

Today your assignment is to say to yourself all day, as often as the Holy Spirit brings this to your mind, *I am so special to God. Jesus will never leave me or forsake me.*

Stop looking for a reason for Jesus to love you because He has loved you from the foundation of the world and will never stop loving you.

I wish I could have coffee with you, look you in the eyes, and say how incredibly proud I am of you for taking these six weeks and standing strong to receive your healing and learning the truth about who you are in Jesus.

We only have two more lessons this week. Then, next week you will get your beautiful robe of righteousness. I love you. We will talk again tomorrow about how much you really are loved!

Week 6, Day 4 — You Are Not Alone!

Many times, rejection brings with it a sense of being alone that can be frightening if we do not take time to hear from the Lord.

I remember when I was so depressed that I was terrified of being alone with my six month old and my two year old. Dave had hired a nanny to come in five times a week, but when her hours were done and Dave was not home, I would panic and page him over and over again. After my deliverance, he said that he would be terrified until he actually walked in the house and saw me and the children.

God bless my husband for not ever thinking of packing up and walking out the door. He deserved so much better, but he stood strong and asked God to heal me. Today, over ten years later, I am not only healed, but I am an evangelist of the gospel, telling every creature there is hope in the name of Jesus.

Hold tight, my sisters, and know that it does not matter what the circumstances are or who it is who has rejected you, because you have a God who loves you and will move heaven and earth to see that you are healed.

Let's go to the Scripture and see what "thus saith the Lord."

Read Isaiah 60:1-16.

Read verse 1 in *The Amplified Bible*. What does this say about circumstances in your life? How are they affected by the Word?

_____

_____

_____

_____

In verse 15, what is the promise that is made to a child of God?

_____

_____

What was the hardest time you have suffered from rejection or betrayal?

_____

_____

If you have not allowed Jesus to speak to you about this situation, take time and pour it all out to Him now and write down what He says to you today, either through the Holy Spirit or through the Word of God:

_____

_____

_____

_____

_____

If you have heard the voice of the Lord about this situation, take a few moments to tell about what the Lord spoke in the past to remind you of your past deliverance:

_____

_____

_____

Hearing the words of the Lord will change your life forever. Let's end with Hebrews 13:5-6: **"For He Himself has said, 'I will never leave you nor forsake you.' So, we may boldly say: 'The Lord is my helper; I will not fear. What can man do to me?'"** Say these verses out loud all day to remind yourself of the truth about who you are to the Lord of lords and the King of kings.

I love you and I look forward to you getting some beautiful new garments and robes next week. You are going to look so beautiful in your new wardrobe from Calvary! Jesus has already paid the check!

Week 6, Day 5 — Yes, He Can Relate to You!

As I read over this week's lessons while preparing for today's lesson, I was amazed at how much the Lord Jesus really loves all of us, His beautiful girls. We are so loved and adored by the King of kings and the Lord of lords. You may be wondering why I continue to say the same things about how we are loved. It's because the Holy Spirit keeps bringing these thoughts to me to remind me of this great truth.

Remember in past lessons I said I desired to have someone who could relate to all of the pain and rejection I have suffered through my life? I mentioned how King David could relate to being rejected by his mother and father, but there is One who can relate to every incident you and I have suffered.

Write out Hebrews 4:14-16:

_____

_____

_____

_____

_____

_____

_____

Jesus can relate to every road you have ever been down because He had to take all of that sin upon Himself at Calvary. Yes, our High Priest did not sin so He could be that final sacrifice for us. However, He can stand with you and say, "I know how such horrific rejection feels.

137

You can make it because I have overcome the world for you, My sweet daughters."

God can take you in His arms and hold you as a loving Father and say, "It is going to be fine because Jesus' blood provided healing for every harsh word or act the devil did to try to destroy your life."

As I write this, I feel a need to say to any women reading this who were supposed to have died many years ago that Jesus has such a beautiful plan for your life and the best is yet to come! Hold your head high and know you are adored by Jesus who is looking at you right now with such intense love that it would melt the sun if He looked into it. Be at peace, knowing this is your final day before we unbutton this robe, discard it, and walk away to never look back.

The Holy Spirit brought back the robe of rejection to my memory and I finally had to acknowledge it in my life. I was getting ready to preach at a Women's Conference, and the Lord had kept my mind concentrated on Mark 10:46-52 for two weeks. Every time I would sit down to study or prepare the sermon I was getting ready to preach, I would come back to these verses. After doing the research and remembering a friend telling me about the different robes of the biblical culture, I kept going back to Mark 10:50.

Read Mark 10:46-52.

Write out Mark 10:50:

_____

_____

_____

In this verse, Bartimaeus threw off a robe before he went to tell Jesus what he wanted. You see, my sisters in Christ, blind men wore robes to tell the people who walked near them that they were blind. Everyone who looked at Bartimaeus knew he was blind by the robe he wore.

What are the things in your life that are screaming that you have on a robe of rejection? Is it your hesitation to step out and make new friends because of fear of rejection? Is it not being honest with your husband about your feelings because of fear of rejection? There are many possibilities. Be honest with yourself. Take a few minutes to answer these questions:

_____

_____

_____

_____

Bartimaeus knew that if he got Jesus' attention, he would not be blind anymore. So he took his blind robe off before standing in front of Jesus. He knew that he was going to see because he was standing before the Messiah and everything was going to be all right.

My sweet sisters, you have to be bold in your prayers and believe just like Bartimaeus that Jesus will relieve you of all pain and rejection you have suffered. (Hebrews 4:16.) We serve a loving God. He will not turn a deaf ear to you when you approach Him today about healing you. He asked Bartimaeus what he had need of.

When I read this for the first time, I thought to myself, *the Lord knew Bartimaeus was blind, so why did He ask him the question?* The Word says in James 4:2, **"You do not have because you do not ask."**

Step out in faith right now and write the rejections you need to be healed of:

_____

_____

_____

_____

I will never forget the morning I was reading Mark 10 again and the Holy Spirit told me to go into my ministry office and shut the door to spend time with the Lord. I went to my office, locked the door, and sat down at my desk, wondering what would happen next. The Holy Spirit spoke to me and said, "Take off the robe." I said, "Lord, what robe are You talking about?" He told me to take off the robe of rejection. I fell to my knees, saying that I thought I had already done this.

Suddenly, it was as if a chain link fence was on my back and I felt the robe of rejection I had worn all of my life. The Holy Spirit told me to stand up and start unbuttoning the buttons of rejection that held this robe on my body. I remember saying that I could not stand and it was as if the Holy Spirit took me by my hands and lifted me up to stand so the robe could be removed.

I stood up with tears streaming down my face, having to acknowledge that I could not remove this robe without Jesus' help. He said, "Unbutton the top button," which represented being molested from age four to age fourteen. He said, "Unbutton the next button," which represented no one in my family noticing all of the anxiety and bed-wetting and other things that accompany such abuse. Next, He told me to unbutton the button that represented being disowned at age thirty and shunned because of my belief in Jesus as the Son of God and all of the years of pain associated with this rejection.

I sobbed so loudly that I thanked the Lord I was alone in my office and that there was no one else in the building. Suddenly, I felt the robe of rejection fall off of me and I felt as light as a feather, electrified with the love of the Father.

My sisters in Christ, it is amazing to have this horrible robe removed from our lives. Next, I heard the Holy Spirit say, "Now, accept the robe of righteousness."

From the bottom of my heart, and even more importantly, from the bottom of my Father's heart, comes the desire for you to be free from this robe of rejection. Allow the Lord to show you the buttons that hold this painful robe on your life. Was it an elementary school teacher embarrassing you in a class full of your peers? Was a button of rejection from a loved one? Was your rejection being the poorest child in the class and never getting invited to a party?

Allow the Lord to walk you through this healing process and show you the significant buttons. You may have to do this alone in your house when everyone is asleep, or if you are single, you can take the opportunity as the Lord leads you. This is your final step in our lesson. Make it a beautiful experience as you step into freedom and finally get into your new wardrobe.

Take a moment to allow the Holy Spirit to help you identify the buttons that are holding this robe together. Write out those buttons in the space below, and allow the Holy Spirit to help you unbutton the robe that has been hindering you. Everyone will have different buttons and the Holy Spirit will help you identify and unbutton them:

_____

_____

_____

_____

I love you and I wish I could grab you and shout with joy as you get rid of this final robe. Be at peace. We will talk again next week. I look forward to taking you on a wardrobe shopping trip using the Word of God as our guide. Again, I love you and I am so proud of you for making it to the end of the journey of disrobing from your past to walk in your future beautifully adorned for the King of kings and the Lord of lords!

Week 7

You Sure Look Beautiful!

"The Spirit of the Lord GOD is upon Me,
Because the LORD has anointed Me ...
He has sent Me to heal the brokenhearted....
To give them beauty for ashes."
Isaiah 61:1,3

Whenever I know I am going to get a new outfit, I must admit I get very excited! Among the many wonderful things Dave does for me, he has always bought me beautiful clothes. I love it when he takes me to buy something new. Even more than I appreciate the clothing, I appreciate all the thought he puts into our excursions. Before we ever leave the house, Dave has already planned which stores we will visit, where we will get a bite to eat, and of course the budget.

Did you know that Someone is always thinking about you and planning surprises for you? Look at what the Bible says:

How precious it is, Lord, to realize that you are thinking about me constantly! I can't even count how many times a day your thoughts turn towards me. And when I waken in the morning, you are still thinking of me!

Psalm 139:17–18 TLB

Dear sister, all of His thoughts toward you are so wonderful, and He truly loves you more than you can imagine. In fact, He enjoys thinking of ways to bless you. He has been doing it throughout eternity, and it thrills Him to see you enjoying His blessings!

When you woke up this morning, your heavenly Father had already been thinking about you and has a plan for your day. He is even thinking about you right now! He knows that for several weeks now, you have been taking off the negative robes that have held you back in life, and that brings great joy to His heart. He is also aware that today you are going to begin learning about the new wardrobe that He designed with *you* in mind! It may be a new concept to you that He chose you and planned a wonderful life for you before you were even born. The Word of God bears witness to this in the following verses:

[In His love] He chose us [actually picked us out for Himself as His own] in Christ before the foundation of the world.

Ephesians 1:4 AMP

We are God's [own] handiwork ... [born anew] that we may do those good works which God predestined (planned beforehand) for us [taking paths which He prepared ahead of time], that we should walk in them [living

the good life which He prearranged and made ready for us to live].

Ephesians 2:10 AMP

What great truths to think on! He picked you out just for Himself, and He has already made arrangements for you to live the good life!

BLING BLING

Referring back to my outings with Dave, there is another thing I appreciate about him. I can always count on him to be honest about how an outfit looks on me. Of course like most women I ask, "Does it make me look fat?" He has learned how to diplomatically steer me toward designs that are the most flattering to me.

We women love to look beautiful, and I believe the Lord Jesus enjoys seeing "His girls" look beautiful as well. I will even go as far as saying, I believe He likes to see us in "bling bling" if that suits our taste. Of course our primary beauty is to come from our hearts according to 1 Peter 3:4, but our Father is an extravagant God. Why the streets where He lives are paved with gold! Did you know that there are twelve special gates in heaven and that each one is made from a gigantic pearl?

Think of how beautiful His creation is here on Earth. From waterfalls, to the Grand Canyon, to the waves crashing on beaches, His creativity is visible everywhere; and each spot has its own unique, intrinsic beauty. You, my dear sister, are part of that creation! Your heavenly Father knows how to dress you so that you look your very best, and He loves to see you shine for His glory. Psalm 35:27 says that He delights in the prosperity of His servants. Why wouldn't that prosperity include a fine wardrobe?

HEAVENLY CLOTHING

Now let us shift our focus to spiritual clothing. This week your Father God has a very special article of clothing to give you, even more special than Joseph's coat of many colors. (See Gen. 37:32.) It is guaranteed to fit and it cannot possibly make you look fat. Let's read about this supernaturally wonderful garment.

> **I will greatly rejoice in the LORD, my soul shall be joyful in my God; for He has clothed me with the garments of salvation, He has covered me with the robe of righteousness, as a bridegroom decks himself with ornaments, and as a bride adorns herself with her jewels.**

Isaiah 61:10

Notice that "garments of salvation" is plural and "robe of righteousness" is singular. One way that we could interpret this verse is that the robe of righteousness is *one* of the garments of salvation. Others might include the garment of praise, clothes of compassion and love, shoes of peace—the Bible uses many references to clothing in relation to our spiritual lives. But the focus of this week's lesson is this robe of righteousness.

What does *righteousness* mean to you? A simple definition is that it means "to be right with God." When a person is born again, that individual immediately becomes heavenly royalty—a king and priest, to be exact:

> **To Him who loved us and washed us from our sins in His own blood, and has made us kings and priests to His God and Father, to Him be glory.**
>
> **Revelation 1:5–6**

Every king has a royal robe, and in the Kingdom of God, that robe is the robe of righteousness. I think it is perfectly plausible that a sort of coronation ceremony is held in heaven when we receive Jesus as our Lord and Savior. Imagine kneeling before the throne as you declare your loyalty to Him. Hear Him as He declares that the price for your sins has been paid in full and that you have been washed white as snow. Now He is ready to place this new robe upon you. Imagine how it feels as He wraps it around your shoulders. Now you are free to arise with your head held high as you are declared to be a king in the royal court of heaven. Glory to God in the highest!

Before we move on, you might be wondering about a crown—doesn't every king receive one? The answer is yes. The Bible calls it the "crown of *righteousness*" and we will each receive it at the Day of Jesus' appearing according to 2 Timothy 4:8. I find it interesting that again, an article of the royal attire has the word "righteousness" attached to it. I believe this is further indication of how important our right standing with God is. May we never take it for granted.

ROYALTY HAS ITS PRIVILEGES

The credit card company American Express has a slogan as part of its ad campaign that says, "Membership has its privileges." That means, of course, that if you are granted their credit card, you can expect certain privileges that are not afforded to the public at large. You have to qualify.

I believe heaven has a similar slogan. When you become a "member" of the Body of Christ, a citizen of the Kingdom of God, you are clothed with the robe of righteousness. This robe entitles you to certain advantages not afforded to people who are not in the Kingdom. The following are only a few of the privileges:

- instant access to the CEO of the universe, Almighty God (Jer. 33:3)

- unlimited resources (Phil. 4:19; 2 Peter 1:3)

- power and authority over spiritual forces (2 Cor. 10:4)

- spiritual weapons, the armor of God (Eph. 6:11–18)

- the assignment of angels to assist and serve you (Ps. 91:11; Heb. 1:14)

- never having to carry the burden of guilt; the ability to instantly receive forgiveness (1 John 1:9)

There are other privileges as well, but I think you get the picture that being the possessor of the robe of righteousness is a very good thing!

INSTANT ACCESS

Let's focus on the first advantage listed, instance access to God. Now when we ladies decide to go shopping, there are usually certain restraints. We may have to hire a babysitter, we may have to stick to a certain price range, and we may not have much time to find what we are looking for.

Or let's say an issue comes up and we need to discuss with a particular individual. In my own life, when I need to talk to Dave about something, I have learned not to just burst into his office unannounced and begin rattling off every little thing on my mind. Now Dave loves me and is more than willing to listen to what I have to say. But what if he is in the middle of an important business deal or if he has an irate customer on the telephone? Or what if he is having a rotten day and his patience is running low? Would any of those scenarios be a good time to barge in to talk about a cute outfit I would like to buy? Of course not.

When it comes to "shopping" for things in the Kingdom of God, however, there are far fewer restrictions. The robe of righteousness on our shoulders gives us unfettered access to Almighty God! That robe entitles you to walk right into the throne room at any time of day or night. You can even crawl right into the Father's lap! You don't have to worry about timing, how you look, how you feel—nothing. He is available to you 24/7.

This reminds me of a famous photograph of John F. Kennedy Jr. taken when his father was president. The president is seen talking on the telephone, conducting what may have been very serious business. Oblivious to the gravity of the Oval Office, John Jr. is seen crawled up under the desk simply enjoying himself. It has been said that President Kennedy was quite comfortable with his children running in and out of the office. To me this vividly illustrates the type of relationship we are to have with our heavenly Father. He might be dealing with urgent, high-stakes world affairs, yet He has no problem with us running right into His presence for any reason at all. It is amazing to think that no matter when we show up, we are never interrupting Him or inconveniencing Him. Imagine that! The King of Glory, the Creator of the universe has an "open door" policy and we are always welcome. He told us so in His Word:

> **Let us then fearlessly and confidently and boldly draw near to the throne of grace (the throne of God's unmerited favor ...), that we may receive mercy [for our fail-**

ures] and find grace to help ... [appropriate help and well-timed help, coming just when we need it].

Hebrews 4:16 AMP

This aspect of our relationship with God has been especially significant to me. When I became a Christian and left the religious cult I was raised in, my biological parents and siblings disowned me. There were so many days when I felt abandoned and lonely. I would lie on the floor asking God to touch me and to help me make sense of the myriad of issues in my life. And you know what? He always answered. Sometimes He spoke to me through His Word. Other times I sensed the gentle voice of His Spirit whispering to my heart. At other times He used His servants to voice an encouraging or instructive word. People may forsake us, but our heavenly Father never will.

Dear sister, what needs are you facing right now?

So many times I hear people say, "Well, I guess all I can do is pray." That comment lets me know immediately that the person does not realize the things that I have just shared with you. Whatever your need, sweet sister, the robe of righteousness that you were given when you were born again authorizes you to enjoy instant access to God Himself. You do not need to make an appointment and you don't even have to sweet-talk a secretary to get in. Location does not matter either. Wherever you are in the universe, you can get into contact with your Father immediately, quicker even than instant messaging your friends. Prayer is the most powerful thing we can ever do on Planet Earth. Simply put, prayer is conversation with God, but through that "conversation," you have the unlimited supply to meet every conceivable need. No, dear sister, never make light of prayer because,

The earnest (heartfelt, continued) prayer of a righteous man makes tremendous power available [dynamic in its working].

James 5:16 AMP

As you meditate upon these truths and they become real to you, you will never underestimate the power of prayer again.

A Dream Relationship

Once I realized that the robe of righteousness entitled me to this type of intensely personal relationship with God, I began experiencing the father/daughter relationship of my dreams. The following verse had a great deal to do with this because it changed my entire perception of God.

For [the Spirit which] you have now received [is] not a spirit of slavery to put you once more in bondage to fear, but you have received the Spirit of adoption [the Spirit producing sonship] in [the bliss of] which we cry, *Abba (Father)*! Father!

Romans 8:15 AMP (italics added for emphasis)

Abba is the Aramaic word for "Daddy." It was the term that Jewish children used to address their earthly fathers. Not just anyone can refer to a man as "Daddy." This term of endearment is reserved only for the very closest of individuals, yet the heavenly Father has revealed that He desires a Daddy/child relationship with every believer. For you and me, dear sister, He desires a Daddy/daughter relationship. I came to know Him in this way through receiving Christ as my Savior and through reading His love letter to me—His Word. He is the One I run to when I need answers to the hard questions in life and He never hesitates to answer. This is the kind of relationship that He wants to have with *you*.

IT JUST DOESN'T SEEM REAL

One thing that each of us has to learn is not to get caught up in our feelings, our emotions. So many times women have said to me, "Jennifer, I do not *feel* this robe," or "I don't *feel* worthy to talk with God," or "I don't do *feel* saved." Women are emotional beings with a complex makeup. We are especially susceptible to feelings due to hormones or simply because God made us to be emotional, nurturing individuals. But that does not mean that our lives have to be controlled by feelings!

It is important to understand that we are triune beings. First and foremost, we are spirit beings who will live eternally. This is the "real" us, the part that is born again when we receive Jesus as our Lord and Savior. We have a soul, which includes our mind, will, and emotions. And we live in a physical body, which the Bible refers to as the "flesh." You probably know from personal experience that feelings can get us into trouble. They are simply unreliable and the enemy can use them to confuse us. The apostle Paul understood this tendency and he addressed it as follows:

> **I have been crucified with Christ ... It is no longer I who live, but Christ (the Messiah) lives in me; and the life I now live in the body I live by faith in (by adherence to and reliance on and complete trust in) the Son of God, Who loved me and gave Himself up for me.**
>
> **Galatians 2:20 AMP**

This verse leaves no room for feelings to enter the equation. Whether you *feel* it or not, Jesus *deeply* loves you. He gave up His very life for you! When it comes to believing the Word of God or some other person, feeling, or circumstance, I choose to agree with the apostle Paul: "Let God be true but every man a liar" (Rom. 3:4). And do not forget, the devil is the "father of lies" (John 8:44 NASB) and he will constantly try to convince you of anything other than the Word. He is especially persistent at trying to get you to doubt your right standing with God because he knows that will undermine your confidence to stand against him. I exhort you, dear sister, do not allow your feelings to control you anymore. Choose to be controlled by the Word of God. The Word says you are covered with a robe of righteousness whether you feel it or not.

A DAILY PROCESS

When I began my walk with the Lord, my soul was extremely damaged and fragile as a result of the abuse and trauma I had suffered. I knew I needed a daily miracle in order for my mind to be restored and made whole. When I learned about the power of the Word of God and became convinced that it was the Truth, I began speaking to my mind every single day. The real me, my spirit, would talk to my soul and tell it to line up with the Word of God. Many, many days I walked the floors of my home early in the morning, instructing my mind what it would and would not think based upon what I read in the Word of God. I spoke to my mind and told it that I was covered with the robe of righteousness. I told it that this meant that God would never deny my request for healing. Based upon Isaiah 53:5; Matthew 8:17; and 1 Peter 2:24; I was healed. I commanded my mind to think on that fact. Dave often awoke to the sound of me quoting the Word of God. He would just smile because he knew that the Word of God was transforming his wife.

Dear sister, you do not have to fix yourself or follow some magic formula to be healed. Understand that the robe of righteousness provides a protective covering for you and it entitles you to complete soundness—spirit, soul, and body. Isaiah 53:5 in the *Amplified Bible* says it this way:

The chastisement [needful to obtain] peace and well-being for us was upon Him, and with the stripes [that wounded] Him *we are healed and made whole.*

(italics added for emphasis)

IN CONCLUSION

Let me say, dear sister, life on earth is truly difficult. After all, we are aliens here; "our citizenship is in heaven." We are merely here on assignment as "ambassadors for Christ." (See 1 Peter 2:11; Phil. 3:20; 2 Cor. 5:20). But you do not have to wait till you get to heaven to enjoy an abundant, blessed, fulfilling life. Jesus said, "I have come that they may have life, and that they may have it more abundantly" (John 10:10). And He taught us to pray that it would be on earth, even as it is in heaven. He would not have instructed us to pray this if He did not intend to bring it to pass.

Do not give the devil the satisfaction of thinking that he can cheat you out of what is rightfully yours. Not because of you have earned it, but because Jesus paid for it at Calvary. Wear your robe of righteousness with your held head high. Put on "the garment of praise for the spirit of heaviness," and allow Jesus to give you "beauty for ashes." (Isa. 61:3.) Take hold of the joy set before you and never, ever forget how very much you are loved, cherished, and celebrated by God Himself. You are and always will be "Daddy's girl."

Before I close, I want to pray for you.

Daddy,

As my sister in Christ works through the final week of our study together, I pray that she would place every concern into Your faithful hands, freeing her arms to put on the robe of righteousness that You have given her. Reveal to her the depth of what that robe means to her personally; and I pray that she would sense Your presence in, around, and upon her. Every time she picks up her pen to write out a verse or to record her thoughts, remind her that she is covered by Your love and that she is righteous before You.

Daddy, You know every minute detail of my sister's life. I ask that You reveal the specific truths she needs so that she can be set free of the destruction wrought by the enemy. May she be like Abraham and not waver at Your promise through unbelief but be strengthened in faith, giving glory to You. (See Rom. 4:20.) Cause everything that the devil has brought against her to be turned for her good and Your glory.

I know it is Your desire that my dear sister be healed of every injury she has sustained, whether it is physical, emotional, or spiritual. Help her to feel safe to run into Your arms and rest there for a while. Help her to receive Your healing love, Your peace, Your strength. Cause her to become all that You have destined her to become.

Finally, Daddy, thank You that You will never abandon nor forsake my dear sister. Thank You for watching over her and for even carrying her at those times when she cannot take another step. Keep her safe until the two of you meet face-to-face. Amen.

Now, as one who has been healed by Jesus Christ, I declare, "You go, girl," and get decked out for your King. I can hear Him now, saying as we do in the South, "My, my. You sure look beautiful!"

Week 7

Accept the Robe of Righteousness

Week 7, Day 1 - Your New Robes

At last, my sisters, we can prepare to get dressed in the robes the Lord Jesus paid for us to put on and look in the mirror knowing the clothes fit and make us look gorgeous. You should feel so much freer and at peace discovering lies the enemy had placed on your life through what I have learned to call "robes." (Take a few moments before you move on and reflect on the goodness of our God and all He has released you from over the past six weeks.)

My reflection is due to a situation a staff member and I had to be involved in. We took a ride in the country to visit a young woman under house arrest because her husband was in jail on serious charges against children. We ministered to this precious young lady and rejoiced that she was reaching out to Christ in the midst of her trauma. We told her that she would be a powerful testimony one day and that it was the Lord's specialty to take a mess and make a ministry out of it.

When we left, I could not help but be humbled by the fact that if it had not been for the grace of God, I would be in an even worse situation. You see, this woman lived in the same neighborhood that I did as a young child and even remembered things about me as a child that I had blocked due to the trauma in my life. When she started telling me things, I could not help but think, Jesus, if I had not met You, I would be in a mental institution or dead.

Taking off the robes of rejection and abuse has been such a blessing to me. This woman said to my team member, "Look at Jennifer over there in a suit and ministering. She sure has changed." Yes, I have been changed through the blood of Jesus, and you have also been changed through His blood. Get ready for your new clothes this week. I know you will look fabulous in them!

Are you viewing things differently since you have been taking off "robes" for the past six weeks?

_____

_____

_____

_____

Write out Isaiah 52:1-2:

_____

_____

_____

Write out Isaiah 62:5:

_____

_____

_____

My dear sisters, you are in the Body of Christ, which is the "Bride of Christ." The Lord desires to come back for His Bride to take us to be with Him in heaven.

I remember getting ready to marry Dave and all of the preparation that needed to be done to be his bride. The gown was supposedly the most important item of the wedding day for the bride. We know that each bride wants to have the most beautiful gown in the world. There was the veil that he would lift to kiss me when I became his wife. Also, I had to get shoes and jewels to match the dress. The day I became Mrs. David M. Kostyal, I wanted to look perfect and take his breath away as I walked down the aisle.

My dear sisters, the Lord already thinks you are the most beautiful bride-to-be. You do not have to spend weeks and months on either a diet or exercise routine. The wardrobe He has in His Word is so incredible and will make you realize you are unmistakably the most beautiful bride in the whole world as you get ready to meet Him face-to-face.

Have you ever thought how your Bridegroom, Jesus, will be dressed as He comes to get you?

Read Revelation 19:11-16.

What will Jesus be riding?

_____

_____

In fairyland, Prince Charming always arrives on a beautiful white horse and rescues the young maiden whom he takes to live with happily ever after as his wife. As a child, I would dream of riding away from my childhood home and having someone listen to the awful things that had been done to me and make them all right.

Please listen closely to what I am about to say to you. We do have a King who is going to return to get us, and He will wipe away every tear and truly make everything all right. One day our Lord and Savior is going to split the eastern sky and we will see our Bridegroom face-to-face if we are not already with Him in heaven. Wow! What a day that will be. Everything that has scarred us or traumatized us and the awful rejection will be gone forever.

You are the beautiful Bride of Christ and He paid the price for your beautiful wardrobe. Get ready to feel like a queen and know you are loved, because you are! Hold your head high and know you are so important to the Lord that He will stop making universes to see that you know you are loved and that He is coming back just for you.

Let's end today's lesson with Psalm 45:13-15, which reveals who you really are:

"The royal daughter is all glorious within the palace; her clothing is woven with gold.

"She shall be brought to the King in robes of many colors; the virgins, her companions who follow her, shall be brought to You.

"With gladness and rejoicing they shall be brought; they shall enter the King's palace."

Week 7, Day 2 - The Robe of Righteousness

According to Second Corinthians 11:2, to whom are believers married?

_____

_____

If you have never known what it feels like to have someone really adore and love you, you need to stop and imagine looking into the blazing eyes of Christ. Look deep into His eyes and see the deep love He has for you.

As I have said so many times, Dave is a wonderful husband, but there were many times he could not mend the wounds in my life or even make me forget them no matter how hard he tried. Even after almost fifteen years of marriage, I go to my foyer or den many nights after Dave goes to bed and cry out to the Lord for strength and healing. I desire to sit at the Bridegroom's feet and get heaven's perspective on the circumstance that is causing me distress.

My sisters, no man on this earth can heal you. In counseling many women, I hear so many who look for their husbands or boyfriends to fill a void in their lives. ONLY Jesus can heal us and set us free to love and be loved. ONLY Jesus can anoint us to be mothers, daughters, and sisters in Christ. ONLY Jesus paid the price for sin that was brought in when Eve doubted if God really meant what He said about eating from the tree in the midst of the Garden. Remember, Adam and Eve made clothes for themselves because they disrobed themselves of their beautiful spiritual clothes that the Lord had given them.

Now, let's put the correct clothes back on and get ready to walk the aisle to meet the King of kings and the Lord of lords. Let's put on our first piece of clothing, one we brides enjoy wearing.

Isaiah 61:10 says, **"I will greatly rejoice in the Lord, my soul shall be joyful in my God; for He has clothed me with the garments of salvation, He has covered me with the robe of right-**

eousness." Wow! We are putting on the "robe of righteousness" and the garments of salvation. Let's look at the definition of these two words we often hear.

What is your definition of "righteousness"?

_____

_____

What is your definition of "salvation"?

_____

_____

According to *Holman's Bible Dictionary*, "righteousness" is the action and positive results of a sound relationship within a local community or between God and a person or His people.[10] Holman defines "salvation" as the acutely dynamic act of snatching others by force from serious peril. In its most basic sense, salvation is the saving of a life from death or harm. Scripture, particularly the New Testament, extends salvation to include deliverance from the penalty and power of sin.[11]

My dear sisters, you are covered by a "robe of righteousness," and you are in right standing with the Lord. He Himself snatched you from the hands of the devil. We have much to rejoice over when we realize what we are placing on ourselves with these new clothes.

Can you imagine if you really realized you are the Bride of Christ? Today many people love to "name drop." I have even noticed this in Christendom. We expect that of Hollywood, but I was surprised when I saw this happening within the Church. Let me say right here and now, my sisters. You are children of God, and you are the "righteousness of God," according to Second Corinthians 5:21. You have beautiful "robes of righteousness" and garments of salvation. You have definitely got it going on!

Today when the devil wants to tell you how bad your life is, how bad you look, or how bad you feel, remember, you have a gorgeous robe and garment that represents all a girl could ever dream of wearing.

Tomorrow we will accessorize and get an understanding of how we really look to our Maker and Bridegroom. I leave you with the scripture from Second Corinthians 6:16: **"For you are the temple of the living God. As God has said: 'I will dwell in them and walk among them. I will be their God, and they shall be My people.'"**

You are the temple of the living God, clothed in the robe of righteousness and in the garment of salvation. You were snatched away from the devil, and he has no more rights to your life in the name of Jesus. Also, you sure look beautiful in your new bridal clothes! We will go shopping again tomorrow.

---

[10] *Holman's Bible Dictionary*, 1194.
[11] Ibid., 1222.

Week 7, Day 3 - More Clothes, Even Shoes

I absolutely love to go shopping and I have never met a woman who doesn't like to get some new clothes, shoes, and jewelry. In fact, even "little women" like to go shopping.

Our ministry buys needy children new clothes and shoes to start out the new school year. I get so tickled to see their sweet little faces when they put on things they like. Their precious eyes just light up and they say, "Mrs. Jennifer, can I have this outfit?" I always say "yes" with a big grin, and when they say "thank you," I tell them the clothes are from Jesus, not me. The partners of our ministry send the money so we can have the honor of taking these children shopping.

When we stand in our new clothes this week, we need to say a big "thank You" to Jesus. Many times when I think about the many things the Lord has done for me, I cannot help but shout "hallelujah" and do a little dance!

Many times in conferences during praise and worship, I may dance and scream, "Thank You, Jesus," because of the opportunity He has given me by healing my mind and my family and giving me new life. Today, my sisters, do not forget to tell Jesus "thank You" in your own way.

My husband Dave is a quiet worshiper. Sometimes I look over at him during a service and tears are just rolling down his cheeks, and I realize that is his way of shouting to the Lord for all Jesus has done for him.

Take time today to tell Jesus "thank You" for all of the things He has disrobed you of and all the beautiful garments He is going to give you.

Write out Isaiah 61:3:

_____

_____

_____

_____

Write out Song of Solomon 7:1:

_____

_____

_____

_____

Did you know that you could get the garment of praise for the spirit of heaviness? I stood on this verse for many years while battling depression. In fact, in my childhood I do not ever remember not being depressed. When I found this verse, I was so happy that I could turn in the spirit of heaviness for a garment of praise. This may seem new to you, but remember, you can apply the Word of God to your life and believe and receive it in the name of Jesus. (Matthew 21:22.)

Many times when I would feel that spirit of heaviness coming upon me, I would scream out that the Lord had given me the garment of praise instead and I would feel that spirit leaving me as I realized all that Jesus had done for me. I am not telling you to be in denial about your circumstances. Tell your problems to Jesus and to your dear sisters in Christ and let Him work them out for your good.

Philippians 1:6 says, **"Being confident of this very thing, that He who has begun a good work in you will complete it until the day of Jesus Christ."** The Lord is not going to abandon the work He is doing in your life. He will complete the work and make you whole in the name of Jesus. Allow Him to do the work and you just rest and enjoy the spa of the Holy Ghost! The Holy Spirit has been exfoliating some things off of you that have been needlessly present for years.

Now, let me talk about those gorgeous sandals He has for you. For many years I did not like to wear sandals because I always felt I had ugly feet due to the fact that my second and third toes are longer than my big toe. In fact, growing up, my siblings used to call me "monkey toes" and I was always ashamed for anyone to see them.

When I married Dave and I knew I had a honeymoon coming, I decided to get a pedicure. I did not wear sandals on my wedding day, because I was not comfortable with my feet. However, I knew I could not wear those wedding shoes the rest of my life, so I decided to do the best I could with these "monkey toes."

Being raised on a farm, I had many callouses and when I went to get my pedicure, I remember them taking the razor and shaving off so much skin that I thought they had removed my feet! It is amazing how pretty my feet looked when all of that old skin was removed and they put a beautiful color pink on my toenails. I remember wanting to wear sandals and I even wore the pedicure foam slippers around for a few hours I was so proud of my new feet!

Now, let's look at the Word of God and see how your feet look to Jesus.

Write out Romans 10:15:

_____

_____

_____

_____

My sisters, according to the Word of God, we are all ministers. Therefore, we bring glad tidings of the good things of Jesus Christ. You have beautiful feet with gorgeous sandals to put on those feet. Now, imagine the gorgeous sandals in the shoe store of heaven!

Many times I have gone into shoe stores to look and saw the most incredible shoes. I knew there was no way I was going to spend hundreds on one pair of shoes because I knew Dave would faint if I did.

I am telling you, these shoes are gorgeous, and remember, they are paid for and you've already had a pedicure. Let's look at one more verse in Ephesians where footwear is discussed.

Write out Ephesians 6:15:

_____

_____

In your opinion, what does it mean to have your feet shod with the "gospel of peace"?

_____

_____

_____

_____

Remember, we have talked about peace in Hebrew, meaning nothing missing, nothing broken. When we have our feet standing on what Jesus has done for us, then we can have peace no matter what is going on or what has happened in our lives. Stand on the Word of God over your life and know that you are shielded with your beautiful robe of righteousness and have the garments of salvation and praise also covering you.

When you look down at your feet, you see them covered with sandals from Jesus that say you are standing on the peace of the Word of God. When you focus on Jesus, everything in your entire life looks different. You are wearing the most beautiful clothes any woman could think to wear.

For years I thought what I wore defined me in the natural. I used to be very intimidated even to go into the nice boutiques and shoe stores to browse. Now that I have on the right spiritual clothes, I realize it does not matter what clothes people have on because they cannot hang with us women of God who have on the robes, shoes, and accessories the Lord has for us.

Enjoy your new clothes! We will get some jewelry tomorrow. I love you! You sure do have pretty feet!

Week 7, Day 4 - Jewels from the King

Isaiah 61:10 says, **"And as a bride adorns herself with her jewels."** When you go into wedding shops, there are jewelry sets that look so pretty for a bride to wear on her wedding day. However, these necklaces, rings, and earrings are not real diamonds, silver, or gold.

The accessories for our gowns the Lord has for us are the best gems in the world. To our God, gold and jewels are only the finest and we will, in fact, walk the streets of gold in heaven. The jewels in the gates of heaven are huge. (Revelation 21:10-21.)

Let's look at the jewels the Lord speaks of in His Word.

Write out Malachi 3:16-17:

_____

_____

_____

_____

_____

_____

_____

Write out Revelation 21:18-21:

_____

_____

_____

_____

_____

_____

_____

_____

Now, what is the thing that the bride loves to show off in her wedding portrait and her friends always ask to see? We know the answer is the engagement ring. The groom spends so much time picking out the perfect ring and is expectantly waiting for his bride to show her approval.

Your heavenly Father has already prepared many jewels for you that actually are so big they are gates. You have the ring of rings waiting and you cannot imagine how beautiful it is! We put so much value on things that do not compare to heavenly things that our Father has prepared for us, His daughters. (Ephesians 3:20.)

I have heard of jewelry stores where you have to have special appointments to visit because the jewelry is so expensive. Only the elite of America or other countries could afford the jewels that are in these stores. Also, I have seen pictures of royal jewelry that companies copy because women like to wear certain replicas of the Crown Jewels. My sisters, if only you could see the beautiful rings, necklaces, and bracelets that your Daddy in heaven has for you.

When the children of Israel left Egypt, they went to their neighbors and asked them for their jewelry as the Lord commanded them through Moses. You see, the Lord loves for us to have jewelry and He can afford the most magnificent pieces. Also, He knows your ring size, wrist size, and ankle size. How good we are going to look in all the different pieces of jewelry He has for us! Go ahead and pick out your favorite size, color, and design. He can have it designed just for you. I cannot wait to see what you picked out or you just may wait for Him to pick it out for you. I allowed Dave to pick my engagement and wedding rings and I was surprised by his taste. I know you will be surprised by Daddy's taste also.

Recently, I took Rebekah to a princess party. I had to get her a crown to wear to that party. We had so much fun picking out that crown. Did you know your heavenly Father has a beautiful crown for you and it is made of real gold?

Open your Bible to Psalm 21:2-3 and you will see that it pleases the Lord to give you your heart's desire and to give you a beautiful crown. He loves you so much and desires for you to feel so special with all of the beautiful robes, garments, shoes, and jewelry He has for you.

You may not be able to see all of this attire now in the natural, but I declare to you it is there. You are the best dressed woman in the States and you are loved and adored by your God and my God. When you walk out to show Him how you look in your new items, He will say how incredibly beautiful you are.

Many times women grow up not hearing how beautiful they are to their earthly fathers. If you will stop and listen, you can hear God saying how beautiful you are and how proud He is of you for taking time out of your busy schedule to spend time with Him in this Bible study.

Remember, the truth will set you free according to John 8:32 and truthfully, you do look especially beautiful today. All day today I want you to continuously tell yourself how beautiful you are and delight in the fact that your Father in heaven has enjoyed seeing you in all of your new clothes, shoes, and jewelry.

Let's end with Revelation 21:4-5: **"And God will wipe away every tear from their eyes; there shall be no more death, nor**

sorrow, nor crying. There shall be no more pain, for the former things have passed away.' Then He who sat on the throne said, 'Behold, I make all things new.'"

Again, my sweet sisters, you look marvelous. Praise the Lord for the new spiritual clothes you have added to your wardrobe this week. We will talk again tomorrow. We are now approaching the end of our journey. Rest in His arms today and know all is well as you trust in the Lord God Almighty to encourage and edify you through His Word, His Spirit, and His people.

Week 7, Day 5 - The New You!

You really made it through this journey with me for seven weeks. I am so proud of you for your steadfastness, perseverance, and diligence to make it until the end. The Word of God changed me forever, and I will be a student of the Word of God forever. In a world without distinct right and wrong, I praise God for His Word that contains all of the answers I will ever need in this lifetime and in the one to come.

The changes you have made as a result of this study will impact you for years. The Holy Spirit promised me that the women who did this study would never be the same in the name of Jesus. Remember, the Word of God is living and powerful and sharper than any two-edged sword, according to Hebrews 4:12. When you have experienced the living Word of God, you will never be the same again.

You have allowed the Word of God to help you remove "robes" that needed to be removed so you could be free to walk in your destiny with only one robe called the "robe of righteousness." You are covered with a robe that man did not give to you and man cannot take away.

I remember when I was growing up how I heard about getting an education because no one could take the degree away from me. Now, after walking with the Lord for ten years, I see salvation, deliverance, and sanctification from the Lord cannot be taken away either by man or by the devil.

We will finish our walk today and again look at one of my favorite Old Testament women who literally saved her entire nation. The woman I am speaking of is Esther. You will see how she changed forever through some preparation on her part and a destiny ordered by the Lord Himself.

My sisters, there is preparation that is needed for you to walk in the destiny the Lord has planned for you. I sense in my spirit as I write this that many of you will see your entire family changed and saved as you stand as Esther did and realize you are called to stand in the gap for the ones you love.

There is one more item I want you to put on that you may have forgotten. We need to smell really beautiful as we get ready to meet our Bridegroom, so let's put on the right perfume. Did you realize you are supposed to smell like Jesus?

I rarely wear perfume because it is one more thing to remember in my busy day. However, as a believer, I desire when people walk by me that they will not only feel Jesus, but they will smell Jesus too.

Read Esther 2:1-17. (I highly recommend that you read the entire book of Esther when you have time.)

How many months did Esther have to prepare to meet the king?

_____

_____

How many months did she spend with perfumes?

_____

_____

Before this Bible study, what did people smell when they were around you? (i.e., people used to smell pride on me because of all of the abuse. I always said to myself that no one was going to hurt me again. Also, I reeked of fear.)

_____

_____

_____

_____

Esther had to change how she smelled and this took six months of intense preparation with perfumes. The ancient beauty process with perfumes was done when Esther built a small charcoal fire in a pit in the floor. Next, a fragrant oil would be placed in the burner and heated. Then Esther would crouch naked over this burner with a robe draped over her to make a tent so the fragrance would surround her. The pores of her skin would open and she would absorb the oil of fragrance in the burner. After six months of this, Esther would smell like the fragrance that burned.

My sisters, what have you been absorbing in your life? What are you continuously putting in your spirit?

Write out Philippians 4:8:

_____

_____

_____

For over ten years I have studied, meditated, and absorbed the Word of God. The "old Jennifer" no longer exists, because I desire for my mind to be the mind of Christ. We know through studying the Word of God that **the Word became flesh and dwelt among us** (John 1:14). How are we going to smell like Jesus? We are going to have to put the Word of God into us so that our old mind-sets are completely gone. You almost have to treat the Word of God like a second language in that you respond with a new language that you are learning.

When Queen Esther was crouched over that coal pit with the fragrance burning, she knew her goal was to smell just like that fragrance because this particular fragrance was what the king loved to smell. I can assure you, the Lord loves His Word even above His name. He loves to be around us when we reek of the Word of God.

Write out Psalm 138:2:

_____

_____

You see, my sisters, the Word of God is the ultimate in all we do as Christians. How have we gotten rid of "robes" that life and the enemy have placed upon us? Of course, we know the answer to that question is the Word of God. How do we get beautiful clothes, shoes, accessories, and even perfume as believers in Christ? Again, the answer is the Word of God. Finally, how do we keep growing and become more like Jesus, our Lord and Savior? The answer is the Word of God.

We must continuously keep our focus on the Word of God so we not lose our correct wardrobe. How will you know you are doing this? When you are walking in obedience to the Lord, you will have perfect peace.

Isaiah 26:3-4 AMP says:

"You will guard him and keep him in perfect and constant peace whose mind [both its inclination and its character] is stayed on You, because he commits himself to You, leans on You, and hopes confidently in You. So trust in the Lord (commit yourself to Him, lean on Him, hope confidently in Him) forever; for the Lord God is an everlasting Rock [the Rock of Ages]."

Keep looking to Jesus for your help and He will never let you down. As we studied earlier, according to Romans 2:11, Jesus is not a respecter of persons. He is not going to give me an abundant life and withhold from you any good thing. Pursue the Lord and the Word as if your entire life depends on it, because in all actuality it does! Enjoy the "new you" and stay in the Word so the "new you" will keep growing and getting stronger every day.

I love you with all of my heart and know the Lord is smiling as we are reading the last few sentences of this Bible study. You are a woman of God and you have an incredible life ahead of you because you have been bought for a price, according to First Corinthians 6:20, and Jesus doesn't buy junk!

Again, I love you. If you ever see me in public, please come and give me a hug. I will rejoice with you for MOVING IN FAITH AND TAKING OFF THE ROBES!

Notes

Notes

Notes

Notes

Notes

Notes

Notes

Notes

Notes

Notes

Notes

Notes

Notes

About the Author

Jennifer Kostyal is a dynamic speaker with a heart for women through the ministries of Transformed By the Word. Through her personal testimony and teaching of the Word of God, she shares her belief in the power of Jesus to heal and make whole.

Jennifer graduated from the University of North Carolina at Wilmington with a Bachelor of Arts degree in Education. She also holds a Bachelor of Theology degree from Mary Shiver Bible College. She is married to David Kostyal and they reside in Wilmington, North Carolina. She says her husband is one of the best presents Jesus has ever given her. They have been greatly blessed with David II, age twelve, and Rebekah, age ten.

Within this ministry she is fulfilling the call to set the captives free as in Isaiah 61. She ministers to people who desire to live abundantly through the power of the blood of Jesus. This ministry is seeing people delivered from darkness to the light of the Son of God in Jesus Christ.

As a Christian, Jennifer is an ambassador of Christ wherever she goes. Her life is a ministry, and in her presence you will find fresh encouragement and a living hope for God's desire to heal His daughters. She truly believes, "Daddy loves His girls"!

www.Transformedbytheword.org
Transformed By The Word Ministries
P. O. Box 10141
Wilmington, North Carolina 28404
910-686-7265